RYAN SPENCE

THE TRIPLE C PROJECT

Find Your Place, Purpose and Peace in a World That Wants to Box You In

Copyright © 2024 Ryan Spence

Ryan Spence has asserted his right under the Copyright, Designs and Patents Act 1988 to be identified as the author of this work.

All rights reserved. No part of this publication may be reproduced, distributed, or transmitted in any form or by any means, including photocopying, recording, or other electronic or mechanical methods, without the prior written permission of the publisher, except in the case of brief quotations embodied in reviews and certain other non-commercial uses.

This book is a work of non-fiction. However, the names and personal characteristics of individuals and details of some events have been changed to disguise identities or protect the privacy of the author's clients. Any resulting resemblance to persons living or dead is entirely coincidental and unintentional. The author of this book does not dispense medical advice or prescribe the use of any technique either directly or indirectly as a form of treatment for physical, emotional or medical problems without the advice of a medical professional.

Identifiers:

ISBN 978-1-7397229-2-0 (paperback)

ISBN 978-1-7397229-3-7 (e-book)

Book editor: Catherine Turner

Book designer: Ines Monnet

Cover designer: Karolina Wudniak

Back cover photography: Palita Mak-Drury

First published 2024 by Take Flight Publishing

For Luca and Rafa

CONTENTS

Note To Reader _____ 1

Introduction _____ 3

1. What the Hell Is The Triple C Project? _____ 10

2. Don't Waste a Minute _____ 30

3. Consistency Beats Intensity _____ 39

4. Finding Clarity through Stillness _____ 54

5. It's Not about Shapes; It's about Self _____ 74

6. Balance Is Not a Destination _____ 83

7. Overcoming Overwhelm _____ 94

8. The Three Stages of Growth _____ 103

9. Connect to Your Inner Child and

   Let Your Feelings Fly _____ 116

10. Find the Keys and Set Yourself Free _____ 123

Acknowledgements _____ 129

Three Requests _____ 131

About the Author _____ 133

Note To Reader

A workbook accompanies this book containing exercises, or mini-projects as I call them, designed to get you up and running in your quest to find your place, purpose and peace.

You can download it for free at iamryanspence.com/project.

Also, look out for, and complete, the project actions at the end of chapters 2-8.

Reading the book alone is a great start, but nothing changes unless you intentionally do the work to make change happen.

INTRODUCTION

I was born to live by the beach. I've always known this. But for a long time I didn't allow myself to admit it.

Why?

Because it's one of those things that people only dream about, right? A pipe dream you have on holiday, when you're sat on a golden beach, listening to the sound of the waves lapping the shore as you sip the coldest beer you've ever had and wonder whether life gets any better than this. *I wish this was my life*, you think, *I wish I could live here*. And you mean it. But deep down you don't believe it could ever happen. And because you don't believe it, it never happens. It's just another unrealised dream in the story of your life.

This is the case with many things in life. We see things, we desire things, we say we want things. But we say it in the same way we asked our parents for that highly coveted but expensive toy at Christmas or that brand-new car when we turned eighteen. We ask with no real expectation of receiving. There's no conviction in our request. We half-ass it because we don't believe that what we are asking for is possible for us. And when we're half-assed in our beliefs and our desires, when we don't truly believe they're possible, we block any potential of those things coming to us.

I decided to stop doing this a few years ago when I launched myself down the personal development rabbit hole in a quest to find myself so I could be myself. And following that decision, things started to change. I stopped deciding that things weren't realistic. I stopped seeing the unrealisation of my dreams as a foregone conclusion. And I began to tell myself repeatedly until I believed it deep within my soul that if I wanted something, I could get it. I just had to figure out how.

I decided to start declaring what I wanted, out loud, sometimes shouting at the top of my voice (in the comfort of my own office of course).

I want this.

I am this.

I desire this.

This will be my life.

I decided to stop allowing myself to be confined to a box, limited by other people's opinions as to what's possible for them, and by extension, for me.

As a state school educated, council estate[1] dwelling, Black British boy, I felt no shortage of people attempting to squeeze me into a prefab box laden with a litany of lazy stereotypes before I'd even reached my teenage years.

If you're from that background, you're not expected to amount to anything. You're not expected to finish secondary school. You're not expected to get a degree. If you do, it won't be a good one. *Set your sights lower,* they think. If you don't end up dead or in jail, you're expected to be grateful to have exceeded their low expectations of what your life could become.

But I never bought into that. Because I came from parents who didn't buy into that. They expected more from my brother and me. But even being from a family that always saw more for me than a dead-end job or life on the streets, their vision of more, like the vision of so many other parents who fought against the odds to succeed, had the same effect of squeezing me into a box. Not a box of lazy stereotypes, but a box marked with the only acceptable options for a child of immigrant parents: doctor, lawyer, accountant. I'm not mad at them for that, even though I pushed back against entering

---

[1] If you're not from the UK, think 'social housing' or 'the projects' for an equivalent visual.

this box for years, because as a parent myself, I get it. People see those careers as stable and secure. And if you're lucky enough to have parents who want what's best for you, they want you to have a level of stability and security that surpasses what they had.

But I didn't want the life my parent's wanted for me.

I knew this early on, but I half-heartedly went along with their plan until my consistently poor grades made it difficult to hide the fact that rather than heading compliantly towards the box they envisioned for me, I was running full speed in the opposite direction.

Their disappointment in my life choices was further compounded when, following a brief glimpse of hope that I was turning my life around after applying for and being accepted into university, I dropped out in my second year to pursue my dream of working in the music business and becoming a pop star.

I was so far from the box by this point that I couldn't see the box. And even though my dreams of pop stardom remained unrealised, and I was perpetually broke, the four years I spent chasing that dream was one of the most alive periods of my life. Because I was doing what I loved. I was going after what I wanted even though I had no fucking clue what I was doing. I had no fear. Well, that's not entirely true. On more than one occasion I woke up in a cold sweat wondering how the hell

I was going to pay rent that week, but I deeply trusted my ability to figure out any obstacle that appeared in my way.

Then somewhere along the way I lost that. As friends gained their footholds on the career ladder, entering a world of regular pay cheques and employee benefits, I became jaded. I was tired of being broke. I knew that any day the big break I'd been working towards could come, but I was tired of waiting for it. What if it didn't come for another year? Another five years? Another ten years? So I did what I felt I had to do. I turned around, headed back towards the box, and conformed.

I gave up on my music dream, got myself a shiny new law degree, and became a BigLaw lawyer. My parents were delighted! And for a short time I was too. After years as a struggling artist, I was 'successful'. I earned more money than I'd ever seen at that point, I worked for one of the biggest law firms in the world, and my future career looked bright. But it wasn't until I had all those things I thought I wanted, that I'd been conditioned to want, that I realised none of it was making me happy. I'd got on this train in pursuit of the money, status, and career prospects, without asking myself whether the things I was chasing were what I really wanted and whether I wanted to go where the train was heading.

If this sounds familiar to you, if you're looking at your own life as you read this and thinking, *Now I understand why I feel so hollow despite everything I've achieved*, then I want you to know you're reading the right book and you're not alone.

I see this same feeling arise in the clients I work with as a high-performance coach. Years of conditioning led them to board a train destined for success, and they continued to ride that train without asking what success actually meant to them, and whether the train was heading to where they wanted to go.

If left unchecked, over time this feeling leads to frustration, unhappiness, and lethargy. And you begin to crave that feeling you used to have, that feeling of aliveness, engagement, and contentedness. That feeling of waking up excited each day because you have a mission, a purpose, something worth fighting for.

I know this because that feeling ate away at me for years, slowly but surely sucking away at my soul until I couldn't ignore it any longer. It was then that I said, 'Enough is enough', stepped off the cliff, and embraced the unknown as I walked away from BigLaw.

I talk about how that happened, the things I had to learn, and the process I had to go through in my first book, *The Triple C Method*®.[2] When I looked back at what I had to do, learn or have to transform from a BigLawyer stuck in survival mode to a BigLaw dropout operating in thrival mode, the three recurring themes in my growth and evolution were the three Cs: clarity, confidence, and courage. These three Cs formed the basis of the method that spawned the book's title.

The ideas and concepts in that book are the foundation of the work I do with my coaching clients and inspired the podcast from which this book takes its name, *The Triple C Project*®. This book builds upon those foundations, providing practical tools to help you fight obstacles that will inevitably arise as you set out on your personal quest to find yourself and change your life.

I wrote this book to help you ignite or reignite the spark within you. To fire up your soul. To make you think differently about who you are, what's possible for you, and what your life could be if you only believed in yourself. I wrote this book to help you find your place, peace, and purpose in a world that wants to tell you what you should do and who you should be. A world that wants to confine you to a prefab box that was never made for you. So get comfortable, keep an open mind, and let's get started.

---

[2] Ryan Spence, *The Triple C Method*® (Sheffield, England, 2022).

1
WHAT THE HELL IS
THE TRIPLE C PROJECT?

So what the hell is The Triple C Project®? And, more importantly, why should you care?

Both are valid questions.

So I'm going to break it down.

Now, if you've read my first book, you'll know what The Triple C Method® is. And if you haven't, I'm not mad because somehow you still managed to find this book and I know you'll be heading straight to the bookstore to grab your copy of the first book because the knowledge I spit in this book wows you so much. Right?

No, really, that was a real question, am I right?

OK, let's continue.

So, if you're new around here, here's a brief history of how I got here (no, not into the world, but here writing this book!).

WHAT THE HELL IS THE TRIPLE C PROJECT? | 11

Before becoming a life coach and yoga teacher, I spent eleven years in BigLaw[3] living the dream of earning a six-figure salary, closing multibillion-dollar deals, and embracing that work hard, play hard mentality. It wasn't my childhood dream to review documents running to hundreds of pages, argue over the same point of law multiple times, and be treated like a disposable resource. But after years of rebelling against the norm in my pursuit of pop stardom, I succumbed to societal conditioning (and the need for cold hard cash), got my law degree (hardest four years of my life), secured a training contract[4] at a top ten international law firm, went to law school (where I increased my alcohol tolerance), then travelled around South East Asia for six months (life-changing), before returning to begin my BigLaw career.

It started with two years as a trainee solicitor (including six months on secondment to the Singapore office), followed by four years in London. And it ended with

---

3 BigLaw is a term used to describe the largest most successful law firms in the world. Typically reserved for firms ranked in the top ten by profit per equity partner but can also be used for firms outside of the top ten that maintain a certain hierarchical, traditional, 'always-on' culture with the billable hours target to match.

4 A two-year training contract in which you rotate through a number of practice areas or 'seats' (usually four rotations, one seat every six months in my case) and hope to obtain a permanent qualified lawyer position at the end of it. It's like a two-year job interview.

seven years overseas as I manifested another secondment to Singapore. By manifested, I mean I told anyone who'd listen that I wanted to go back to live in Singapore, so when a spot opened up, I got the call. Shout about what you want, reader; you never know who will hear your call.

In the beginning, I loved my job. Well, love is probably a bit strong. I liked it though. The work was challenging but enjoyable and I had some fantastic experiences. Like the time I ended up flying business class to Sydney, Australia, a couple of weeks before Christmas on a business trip with long-standing clients who are poster boys for the phrase 'work hard, play hard'. After having a messy night out in Sydney to celebrate a successful week, I rocked up to the airport seriously hungover (if you saw my credit card statement, you'd understand why) and was met with the welcome surprise of an upgrade to first class for the return leg. Woo-hoo!

I met some fantastic people, many of whom I'm still in touch with now. And perhaps the biggest deal for a working-class guy from a council estate who was accustomed to being perpetually broke, I had money! I could do silly things like pay rent, go out for dinner at a restaurant without worrying whether my card would bounce, and get a black cab home.

I was doing the things you're supposed to do as a high-flying junior finance lawyer. I was on that corporate train picking up pay rises, prestige and promotions along the way. To the external world I was a success!

But at some point, something changed.

And it took the birth of my first child for me to finally admit what that something was. I looked at the life that would lie ahead for me if I stayed on the train – the late nights, the cancelled weekends and holidays, the expectation to be on 24/7 – and I admitted to myself that I didn't want that life. The admission was a quiet whisper at first, but one particular incident turned that whisper into a roar.

The demands of the job, and the presenteeism culture perpetuated by certain partners, meant I frequently missed getting home in time to put my newborn child to bed, something I desperately wanted to be able to do.

So I started working from home one day per week to ensure there would be at least one day I'd be around to enjoy this bonding moment with my son. This wasn't a unilateral decision. I discussed it with the partner I worked for, assuming as a relatively new father he'd understand, and a verbal agreement was reached.

All was fine for a few weeks until one day, there was a problem.

As I wrapped up my workday, I sent my usual email to the team letting them know I'd be working from home the next day.

I left, headed to the bus stop, and as the bus made its way down Collyer Quay, then on to Fullerton Road as it crossed the Singapore River I did what I always did, I checked my emails.

'We need to talk.'

That was the response from the partner to my earlier email.

Ominous. I mean, no one likes to receive a 'We need to talk' email. Its brevity and unclear connotation make it probably one of the most anxiety-inducing emails you can receive from your boss.

I felt that familiar anxious feeling arise within me as I wracked my brain to think what we could possibly need to talk about. But in my mind, I'd done nothing wrong, so I walked myself off the ledge and tried to convince myself everything was cool.

It wasn't.

The next day I worked from home as planned and the day after that I headed into the office to face the music. Shortly after arriving at my desk, my boss called me into his office and gave me this whole spiel about how my working from home was a problem. And to add to that, my failure to be sitting at my desk by 9 a.m. every day was also a problem.

Now this confused me. See I'd rarely been at my desk by 9 a.m. since I started my career. I was there if I needed to be, but 9:30[5] was more my vibe, and it had never been a problem. I mean, if you work in BigLaw or any demanding corporate role, you know that you're not signing up to a nine-to-five gig. The advances in modern technology mean you're now expected to be available 24/7, so whether you're sitting at a desk at 9 a.m. or on the bus into the office, it shouldn't matter.

Feeling aggrieved as well as confused, I said as much to the partner. Out loud.

It didn't go down well at all. My failure to sit down, shut up, and accept I was wrong apparently meant that I didn't have the right attitude. I believe the words 'I'm disappointed in your attitude, Ryan' were said.

Now I was pissed!

It felt like when you do something as a kid and you know your parents are mad, but they pull the 'I'm not mad, I'm just disappointed' trick on you. Except, this wasn't my parent and I wasn't a kid.

---

[5] OK, full transparency, on some occasions this may have stretched to 9:45.

But not wanting to escalate the situation and, quite frankly, wanting it to be over, I kept my cool and simply said, 'Well, I get everything done and no one can question my commitment.'

'Well, some people are' was the response.

Now I was really mad.

I thought of all the sacrifices I'd made for the firm over the years. The holidays I'd missed or worked on. The missed bedtimes with my son. The weekends I'd sat glued to my laptop or iPhone, failing to be present with my family. The social events I'd missed. The multiple nights I'd slept with my phone under my pillow so I didn't miss an email or a call on a deal. The times I'd worked from my sickbed.

Yet, because I wanted to have a life outside of the job, to be a present father, my commitment was being called into question.

WTF?

But it got worse.

As I again made the point that working from home was necessary to ensure I would see my child, more fuel was doused on my raging anger.

'Everyone else has kids,' he said as he gestured down the corridor of the office. 'What makes you so special?'

There are times in any argument when you have to make a call. Do you use your rage to fuel the continuation of the argument and risk saying something you'll regret, knowing it will only give you short-term satisfaction and you'll fail to change the person's mind?

Or do you walk away?

I chose to walk away. And that anger never really left me until the day I left the firm.

But even with all of that, I stayed for a good few years beyond that moment. I felt betrayed. I felt angry. I didn't see how I could have an enjoyable future at a firm that treated me that way after I gave it so much. Yet, the thought of leaving terrified me!

It's like when you're invited to a party, but when you arrive the vibe is wack. You stick around in the hope it'll get better. And even though it doesn't, you've now been there so long that you don't want to leave in case it gets better. Can you relate?

In my case I'd been at this particular party for years. Everyone on the outside was impressed that I'd been invited, but they didn't know that the host wasn't great and expected you to give everything you had to make the party jump while giving you the bare minimum in return.

Spoiler alert!

Obviously, I eventually escaped from the party. If I hadn't, I wouldn't be sitting here writing this book. And I can now look back at that time through the lens of someone who's done a lot of inner work to shed the layers and conditioning that kept me at the party I didn't want to be at for far too long.

In looking back, I've been able to deconstruct what was going on for me back then, what it eventually took, what I had to do, and who I had to become to get from where I was to where I am now, physically, mentally and spiritually.

And when I cut right down to the foundation of that transformation, there were three pillars that supported, and still support, my growth and transformation from the angry, unhappy and unfulfilled BigLaw lawyer to the freewheeling, creative, BigLaw dropout writing this book. Those three pillars are:

- ☑ Clarity
- ☑ Confidence
- ☑ Courage

Also known as The Triple C Method®.

Wherever I looked on my quest to leave the law and embark on a mission to positively impact people's lives, these three Cs were ever present, providing structure and direction, and allowing me to go where I'd feared to go before.

As I became clearer on how these three Cs helped me, and I started to see how these three Cs helped my coaching clients, The Triple C Method® began to take shape and ultimately become the foundation that underpins the work I do to guide clients back to who they are so they can stop living as who they're not.

Clarity

Clarity is key. It was key to my journey because, without knowing where I was going, how would I know when I got there? How would I know that I was even on the right path? That's very much how I felt for a large period of my time in BigLaw. I didn't go into BigLaw with any love of law particularly. But I'm not gonna lie, I didn't hate it the whole time I was there. I enjoyed it. Initially, it was nice to be earning money. It was nice to be in an environment where you're working with intelligent people, sharing ideas, and feeling challenged. But it wasn't where I wanted to be and it wasn't what I wanted. I never stopped to question that because on the outside looking in, I was successful, and you don't walk away from that. You just suck it up, right? So getting clarity was a really important factor for me. There were three questions I had to ask myself, and which I still ask myself now as I continue to progress on the path that I'm on. I also ask my clients these questions, and I hope that you will write them down and start asking yourself these questions too, particularly if you're not quite sure you're where you need to be or want to be.

The first question is about you: Who are you? What is it that you like? What are your values? What excites you? Really sit down and think about that. For example, for me, autonomy is a core value. I want to be able to do what I want, when I want, with whomever I want, wherever I want. And that's not really congruent with being in the BigLaw environment where you're expected to be on call 24/7, where in some corners there's still an expectation of presenteeism, where you're literally at the beck and call of the partner or partners you work for. So it's no wonder that I wasn't feeling like I was in the right place. What are your core values?

The second question asks, what do you want? I remember being asked this by my very first coach. I was at a crossroads, knowing I'd be leaving the firm but unsure what I wanted to do next. At first I gave the answers I thought I should give, like 'I want to move in-house' and 'I want to stay in law but change practice area', a litany of law related answers that, had I acted on them, would have put me back on the same train I desperately wanted to get off. of knowing I was in law and doing things around law and that sort of thing. She noticed this and challenged me saying, 'Strip everything away, all the 'shoulds' and expectations. Now, tell me, what do you want?'

I realised that I'd never really asked myself that question before. And when I stopped to allow the dreams and the ideas that I'd dismissed as not being realistic to come to the fore, what I wanted felt powerful. Not just see it in my mind, I could feel it in my body and deep in my soul. Then from nowhere I heard myself say 'I want to do something in yoga and wellbeing so I can help people that are stuck like me. As the words left my mouth I instantly felt lighter. It was as if a backpack laden with bricks had suddenly been removed from my shoulders. Answering that question, What do you want?, from my gut, my soul, my inner knowing, set me on path that I continue to walk down to this day. So I encourage you to take the time to ask yourself this question often. Because what I see in my work is that we're quick to say what we don't want, what we hate, and to complain about our lot in life. But how often do you stop to really drill down into what you do want? How often do you envision that and paint a vivid picture of what your life could be?

The final question for clarity asks, why do you want it? The reason this question is important is because when you're shaking things up, when you're going against the grain, when you're pushing back against the status quo, undoubtedly, you're going to come up against some resistance, which can be external resistance – external resistance from people who don't understand what you're doing, who think you should stick with what you know, who don't want you to succeed – or it can also be internal, such as fear or discomfort that builds up inside of you, that questioning of yourself, *Can I do this?* There are limiting beliefs that want to keep you thinking small. But if you know why, if you've connected to your reason for doing it, what I call your mission or your purpose, that's what will keep you going. I tell a story in chapter 7 of *The Triple C Method®* and revisit it in chapter 8 of this book, about social media and my initial fears of sharing online in the early days of my entrepreneurial path. And the phrase I keep playing in my mind whenever those fears arise is *service over ego*. What am I doing here? Am I doing it for my own ego? Or am I doing it in service of something bigger? Asking yourself why you want what you want will help you to keep pushing forward when things inevitably get a little bit tricky.

Confidence

Confidence is looking at what you want and having the belief that you can actually get it, that it is possible for you. You can work through clarity answering all the questions and say, 'Yeah, I really want this, and this is why I want it; I'm all-in. But if you don't truly believe deep within your soul that what you want is possible you won't get it because you won't do all that's necessary to get it. This was my experience as limiting beliefs held me back for so long. And it was only once I challenged those beliefs and let them go that my confidence started to grow. For example, without breaking through those beliefs and growing my confidence I never would have become an author.

Since I was a kid, I've always wanted to write a book. The dream of holding my very own book in my hands and having people tell me how much my words changed, helped, and entertained them was a recurring one. It was always there, deep within me flickering away like a flame. For years I didn't write a thing, not a blog, not an article, and certainly not a book. I would tell myself I was too busy, that I'd get to it when I had more time, but really I was procrastinating, and I was procrastinating because I didn't believe I could do it. I didn't have the confidence in myself to believe that people would want to read what I wrote. So I didn't write. I didn't speak my mind. When I started on my personal development quest and left BigLaw, I found my creative spark again and started to not only write but also share my writing online. With every share, every comment, every message of support, my confidence as a writer grew, but it took a coach to unlock the cell door blocking the final bit of my confidence that was stopping me from standing up to be counted as an author. And once that final piece of the confidence puzzle was in place, I wrote *The Triple C Method*®. I knew nothing about writing, publishing and launching a book, but my coach helped me see that I didn't need to know everything to start. She showed me that starting to write would build my confidence, which would give me the belief and self-trust that I could figure it out the process along the way, which would encourage me to continue writing, which would in turn make me a better writer and further boost my confidence. See, the thing about confidence is that it isn't built by willing yourself to be confident; it's built by starting the damn thing because you have a deep-seated 'Why', and then trusting that you can figure out the 'How' along the way.

Courage

And the final C of The Triple C Method® is courage.

Courage is taking action, bold action, to get or achieve the thing you want. To continue my author journey analogy, whereas confidence got me writing and believing, it was courage that got me to release my book to the world. See, you can sit, theorise and get really clear about the thing you want, and you can create your vision board, journal on it, and visualise it to build your confidence that you can do it. But if there's going to be any chance of you getting the thing, you've got to take action, and that can be terrifying! It's one of the hardest things to do. Clarity and confidence can largely be gained in silence, amidst the shadows where no one can see what you're doing, what you're striving for. They're broadly focused on the inner work whereas courage requires you to step out of the confines of your mental fortress and enter the arena. You have to do something. And if you do something, people are going to see what you're doing. And once you're in the arena, with people watching, the vision you created for yourself and the actions you envisaged you'd need to take to make that vision a reality become real, then it's scary. Your own deep-seated insecurities that you thought you'd dealt with return to haunt and heckle you. That inner critic has you saying things like:

I'm not good enough.

Who am I to be …?

What if I fail? I'm surely going to fail.

People like me don't achieve things like this. What was I thinking?

And as if that wasn't enough, you also have to contend with other people's agendas and opinions and have the courage to push back. So you need the courage to be on the offensive (to take action) and the courage to roll with the punches and be on the defensive (to deflect criticism).

But as I found and my clients find, once you have that courage, you feel like a superhero. You feel you can do anything. You feel you can take any action, any step, to achieve what you want to achieve and get to where you want to get to.

So how do you go about building that 'superhero saving a child from a burning building' courage?

Well, have you ever built Lego? My kids love Lego and I do too! I love sitting at the kitchen table with a new Lego set and working with them to build the thing. The image on the box of the thing you're building looks amazing, but as you flick through the instruction guide, parts of the process can look daunting. So what do you do?

You don't get intimidated by the enormity of the task ahead of you. You start with the easiest part of the process. Then you move to the next, and then the next, adding Lego piece to Lego piece. And before you know it, time has flown, and the model that looked so daunting to build starts to take shape before your very eyes.

This is how you build courage. It's a concept I call Courage Stacking.

I talk more about Courage Stacking in my last book, *The Triple C Method®*, but essentially Courage Stacking is taking the bigger goal or vision you have for yourself, the one that scares you, and breaking it down into bite-sized actions. Then you take the smallest, easiest step, the step that almost seems too easy. After that, you take the next smallest step, and then the next, stacking courageous step on top of courageous step. And as you make progress towards your goal, you start to realise how far you've come, as you continue to do things that seemed so scary when you started, almost without a second thought. Because each action, each courageous step, is like laying a brick until one day you find you've built a nice big courage wall that sits between you and your fears. And this wall also serves as a reminder, a wall of evidence, that you have done and can do big, hard, scary things.

That's a brief recap of The Triple C Method®, which explains the "The Triple C" part of this book's title. But where does 'Project' come into it? Why the hell is this book called *The Triple C Project*®?

Well, one definition of 'project' is an individual or collaborative enterprise that is carefully planned to achieve a particular aim. And that's what the podcast, and now this book, is. An effort, an enterprise, carefully planned to achieve a particular aim. And that aim is to help you break free of the box you're trapped in and escape your mental cell of self-limitation so you can move from survival mode to thrival mode, from a life of lethargy to a life that's Lit!.

It's a project designed to raise your ambition and help you see that you don't have to do what you've always done and you don't have to be who you've always been.

It's a project created to help you see:

You don't have to let your dreams die.

You don't have to give up on your goals.

You do have choices.

And by gaining clarity, boosting confidence, and building courage, you can become more of who you are and who you're meant to be, rather than defaulting to who you think you should be and retreating to live life in a box that wasn't created for you.

This isn't a book that guarantees you the world. It doesn't give you the blueprint to wealth beyond your wildest dreams (if you have that blueprint though, call me).

I don't make outlandish claims that by reading this book you'll 10x your income, rise to the pinnacle of your career, or live a stress-free life.

What I do guarantee is that once you've read this book, you'll think differently about yourself, your life, and what's possible for you. The lessons in this book helped me find myself and my purpose after years of trying to squeeze into a box that wasn't made for me.

They helped me recognise that sleeping with my phone under my pillow or sitting in front of a computer screen for eighty hours a week didn't have to be my life. They helped me see possibilities I never imagined and release everything that was holding me back from getting after them.

But a book is static. It can't possibly speak to the specifics and peculiarities of your unique situation. So I encourage you to read with an open but critical mind, taking what serves you and leaving what doesn't.

There's no right or wrong way to approach this book. Dive in wherever your curiosity takes you. Read from the middle or the back. Think of it as a choose your adventure because this is your adventure. Your life is your biggest adventure, and you shouldn't settle for living it in lethargy when you could be living it Lit!

2
DON'T WASTE A MINUTE

But will I be too old?

It was a cold, wet night in the lecture theatre of Birkbeck College, the University of London college where I got my law degree. It was the first week of my first year. At the end of the lecture I approached the lecturer to enquire about the chances of pursuing a career in law at, what I believed, was an advanced age.

By that stage of life I'd already failed my GCSEs[6], failed my A-Levels[7] (twice!), signed a recording contract that went nowhere, got into and dropped out of university, moved to London, bagged a dream job at a record company (dream in relation to everything except the

---

6 General Certificate of Secondary Education: an academic qualification in a range of subjects typically taken by 14-16-year-olds in England, Northern Ireland and Wales.

7 Advanced Level: an academic qualification that was typically taken by 16-18-year-olds after completing their GCSEs.

money I was being paid), and lived and broken up with my long-term girlfriend.

And these are only the things I'm prepared to share in this book!

Let's just say I'd lived a little.

I wasn't a fresh-faced student straight out of college. I was what some might call a serial dropout. Bright in mind but with no evidence of an ability to apply that mind to the rigours of a legal career. The product of a council estate upbringing and state school education with no connections to teach him how to find, never mind climb, the ladder to success.

But the thing I was most concerned about was whether any firm would take me on due to my age.

How old was I? Well, it sounds absurd to say it now, but I was all of twenty-eight!

This is how conditioning works. It starts from birth. You're expected to hit certain milestones at certain ages. By what in the old days you might call royal decree, you're expected to walk and talk by a certain age. You're expected to be able to read and write by a certain age. And these expectations never end. You're expected to go to a certain school, get certain grades, attend a certain university, and leave in your early twenties ready to take on that graduate job in the corporate world that will have you set for life.

It's as if you've been put on a train heading to a promised land called Success. When that train arrives at each stop along the way, you're expected to have achieved specific things and hit specific milestones. And if you haven't hit those milestones, if you don't stay on that train until it reaches its final destination, if you don't follow the path mapped out for you, you're seen as a failure.

Don't own your own home yet? Failure!

Not married? Failure!

Don't have 2.4 kids and a two-car garage? Failure!

Don't have the right salary, job title, or status? Failure!

So, although it seems ridiculous to me looking back, it's no wonder I questioned whether I had a future in law given my advanced years (it still makes me laugh to write that).

My lecturer looked at me quizzically, not quite sure what to make of my question. But rather than tell me I was being silly for asking such a thing, she indulged me.

Lecturer: How old are you?

Me: Twenty-eight, but when I finish my degree, I'll be thirty-two.

Lecturer: And?

Me: And I'll be competing with graduates ten years younger than me. So why would anyone hire me?

Lecturer: I've been doing this a long time. You'll be fine.

And that was it. I stood rooted to the spot, pondering her matter-of-fact response as she walked away.

As silly as it sounds now, I bet you've experienced similar feelings, thoughts, or concerns at certain points in your life. You're likely experiencing them now. Maybe you sailed through life hitting all the right milestones at the right time like some child prodigy who just can't help acing every test. But none of that brought you the feeling of joyful accomplishment that you thought it would. So now you're feeling stuck, wondering what it was all for while the dreams you once had lie dormant inside of you. And each time you feel a sense of longing, a desire to relight the spark and chase those dreams, you suppress that feeling, believing that ship has sailed, and the time to pursue them has gone.

Or maybe you're like me: you chased a dream, one that made you feel alive! But weighed down by societal expectations of what success means, and the need to make money, you gave up on that dream, changed course, and followed the well-trodden road to success. And even though you've now achieved the six-figure salary, the prestigious name on your business card, and a reputation as someone who's going places, you too are silently questioning what it was all for, but you feel like you have to suck up the unhappiness and lethargy this 'successful' life has brought you.

Whichever camp you fall into, I want you to do something for me right now: STOP!

Stop telling yourself your time has passed and that where you are now is where you'll always be.

Stop telling yourself that this is the life you chose and you have to accept it.

Stop telling yourself you're too old and too far gone to follow your dreams.

Here are some stats about some ordinary people you might have heard of who never stopped chasing their dreams and went on to do or achieve extraordinary things at a much later age than twenty-eight!

Harrison Ford was working as a carpenter and didn't get his big break as Han Solo in *Star Wars* until he was thirty-four years old.[8]

Vera Wang worked in the fashion industry for almost twenty years before launching her debut line of bridal gowns at age forty.[9]

---

8 Steve O'Brien, 'The Remarkable Story of How Harrison Ford Won the Part of Han Solo', *Uk.movies.yahoo.com*, 2022 https://uk.movies.yahoo.com/movies/remarkable-story-harrison-ford-han-solo-130342666.html, accessed 4 July 2024.

9 Alison Beard, 'Life's Work: An Interview with Vera Wang', *Harvard Business Review*, 2019 https://hbr.org/2019/07/lifes-work-an-interview-with-vera-wang, accessed 4 July 2024.

Helen Mirren was acting for years but didn't get her first Oscar nomination until the age of 61 (and she won).[10]

Samuel L. Jackson didn't get his breakout role as hitman Jules Winnfield in *Pulp Fiction* until he was forty-five years old (and what a role that was!). [11]

Now as inspiring as these stories can be, there's always a tendency to look for reasons why someone else's life is different and why what they did, what they achieved, would never work for you. Maybe you even tell yourself, *Yeah that's cool, but I don't want what they have; I don't want to be famous*. But I don't share these stories because I think we should all strive to be famous movie stars. That's not it at all. This isn't about becoming famous. This is about living your life. This is about trying to get what you want and dream about. This is about finding the thing that makes your heart sing and not stopping until you've made it happen. This is about arriving at your deathbed without any regrets as to what

---

10 Charlotte Chilton, '40 Celebs Who Didn't Catch Their Big Break until Later in Life', *Men's Health*, 2019 https://www.menshealth.com/entertainment/g28721959/celebrities-big-break-later-in-life/?slide=10, accessed 4 July 2024.

11 https://www.menshealth.com/entertainment/g28721959/celebrities-big-break-later-in-life/?slide=3, accessed 17 July 2024

could have been. This is about not wasting a minute of this wild, wonderful, precious life you have.

We're all going to die at some point. That's not a morbid statement; it's simply a fact of life.

Speaking of death, did you know that the global life expectancy is 70.8 for men and 76.0 for women? [12] For the UK, it's 80.61 for men and 83.97 for women. For Singapore (where I lived for seven years before leaving BigLaw), it's 82.13 for men and 86.42 for women.

Now let's say you're healthy, privileged, have no genetic diseases, are fortunate to avoid being a victim of violent crime, and don't frequently partake in high-risk activities like skydiving or bungee jumping. You might expect your life expectancy to be above average. So with the ever-increasing advances in modern technology and the growing body of information about human health and the treatment of diseases, let's be generous and say you may live well into your 90s.

How much time do you have left?

I made it easy for you to visualise that with a simple boxes of life chart. It's in the workbook that accompanies this book and which you can download here.[13]

---

[12] Worldometer, 'Life Expectancy by Country and in the World (2023)', *Worldometers.info*, 2023 https://www.worldometers.info/demographics/life-expectancy/, accessed 5 July 2024.

[13] iamryanspence.com/project

Got it?

OK, now as you can see, each box represents ten years of your life, and within each box is a line representing a year. Now take a pencil or your favourite colouring crayon and shade in the sheet to match the age you are right now.

What do you see? Well, if you're a glass-half-empty kinda person, you're probably freaking out at how much time has passed and how little time you have left. But chill, that's a good thing. Not the freaking out part, but having a visual representation of the passage of time.

So now I invite you to take a moment and notice how it feels to look at the amount of time you've lived and the amount of time you may still have left to live. What comes up for you in your mind, body and soul?

Think about how you've spent your time today, last week, last month, last year. Then ask yourself, *If I knew then what I know now, how would I want to have spent that time? Would I have spent any of it differently?*

Now look at the unshaded part of the sheet, the time yet to pass.

Ask yourself, how do I want to spend that time? Think about the places you want to go, the things you want to see, and the people you want to see them with. Think about what lights you up. Maybe it's that time you danced through the night barefoot on the beach at your best friend's wedding, or the time you had an amazing dinner with a friend where you talked until the restaurant staff began cleaning up around you, or the time you went to the movies with your kid and laughed until your sides hurt.

How could you do more of that? And how would life be different for you if you did?

See the thing is, the time will pass anyway. And it can pass in a haze of doomscrolling social media and sacrificing everything at the altar of the next pay rise, bonus or promotion. Or it can pass with you being intentional about what you want and focusing on how you can best spend the time you have left to get it.

The clock is ticking, my friend. And my job, my mission, is to help you ensure that you make the most of every minute and live life Lit!

Project Actions

- ☑ Complete the boxes of life chart
- ☑ Stick the chart somewhere you'll see it daily
- ☑ Answer the boxes of life chart questions

CONSISTENCY BEATS INTENSITY

I've always been an all-or-nothing kinda guy. When I decide to do something, I go all in and it's all I can think about. I remember when I decided to start my first podcast, *The Yoga Den Podcast*. I binged a ton of podcasts, making notes on what I loved and what I didn't, and agonised over the name, the artwork, and the intro and outro music.

I researched and bought the best gear possible, even though I really didn't need to, because I knew that once I had money on the line, I wouldn't let the fear of putting myself out there stop me from taking the leap.

And once I started the show I went hard!

I committed to putting out an episode every week. One week a technical issue meant my guest interview failed to record. I considered skipping a week, but I was in so deep, and so committed to the process, that

I pushed past my fear and reluctantly recorded and released a solo episode to plug the schedule gap.

I was determined to make each episode perfect. I followed the podcasters I listened to and tried to match them in terms of their marketing and promotion efforts. I poured hours of time I didn't really have into editing the audio and the transcripts. I was intense and relentless in my quest to be a successful podcaster, whatever that meant.

But I was in too much of a hurry. And my impatience meant that instead of taking my time and allowing the show to develop in its own way over time, I kept pushing harder and faster to get to where I wanted to be.

I was a big burning ball of podcasting intensity.

And that intensity eventually impacted my consistency. After sixteen episodes, which included a time span that involved an international relocation from the tropics of Singapore to the brutal cold of the UK with two kids during the pandemic lockdown, I was burntout. I needed a break. And even though I didn't want to take one, I didn't want to stop the show, my body was telling me I didn't have a choice.

So reluctantly I took one.

My intention was to take a month. Enough time to find a place to live, get set up, and recharge my batteries. How naïve was I? That month ended up becoming a year! And during that one-year hiatus, I began to see how the way I'd run the podcast wasn't an isolated incident; it was the way I'd done many things in my life. As someone once said, the way you do one thing is the way you do everything, and that was true for me whether it be podcasting, boxing, yoga, or BigLaw.

And as the penny dropped, and a pattern emerged, the mantra 'Consistency beats intensity' began to circulate in my mind.

So what do I mean by that, and how does it apply to you?

Well, let me paint a picture for you.

Your job is demanding. It's literally taking over your life. And even though you're over it and would rather be doing something else, anything else, you feel you don't have time to do so.

You have several ideas of things you'd like to do, skills you'd like to acquire, and rabbit holes you'd like to go down. But at the end of the day or the end of the week, literally all you want to do is:

- ☑ Go out, party hard, and drink away the pain, before heading home exhausted and passing out in a drunken stupor; or
- ☑ Crash on the sofa, binge-watch Netflix, and shovel copious amounts of junk food into your mouth,

- ☑ all to numb the pain of the life you've found yourself living; or
- ☑ Take the edge off with a glass of wine, which far too frequently becomes two glasses, three glasses, or on some occasions, an entire bottle.

That's all you have the energy for. It's hard to muster up the strength to do anything else as your job has taken over your life. And although you dream of having a week, a day, or even an hour to focus on yourself, what you want, what you need, in your head that's unrealistic. You just don't have the time.

Sound familiar?

You're not alone.

It's a common complaint I get from clients I work with. They want to do things like:

- ☑ write a book
- ☑ start a business
- ☑ get a master's degree in a subject they're passionate about

They visibly light up when I get them to talk about all the things they'd love to do and try to achieve. But their demeanour changes to one of resignation as they say, 'But I just don't have time to even look into that. My work is all-consuming; life is all-consuming.'

Like my client Martha (not her real name). Martha was a BigLaw lawyer, but when we got down to it, it was clear she wanted to be a writer. She had history as a writer, but like many lawyers I know, once she got on the BigLaw train, all that creativity somehow disappeared in a sea of billable hours, urgent deadlines, and office politics.

Martha's story, like so many stories I've been privileged to hear, was that her job was demanding, her family life was demanding, and with all the day-to-day pressures of life, she didn't have time to read for pleasure, let alone write.

I listened and smiled as she spoke.

I smiled because I knew from experience that as long as she held that belief, a belief that felt very real to her, it would become a self-fulfilling prophecy. It sounds trite, but if you believe you don't have time, you won't have time.

I also knew that belief didn't have to be true if she didn't want it to be. It's just that when you're in the thick of the story you're telling yourself, it feels so real that it becomes hard to step back and objectively look at the situation.

This is why I love being a coach – I have the luxury of being detached from the situation so I can see what clients can't see. I watch and listen with curiosity and pull the threads the client doesn't see or is afraid to pull so we can get to the core of what's really going on.

I knew the story Martha was telling herself wasn't true. See, we can always make time to do the things that we want to do, we just have to recalibrate our expectations to meet the time we have available. When Martha said she didn't have time, what she meant was she didn't have the time she wanted to have, and thought she needed, to sit down and focus on writing. To be a real writer she believed she had to have a luxurious amount of time to write, multiple hours per day at least. And because she believed she didn't have that, and she couldn't see a way to ever have that, she didn't write.

It's similar to what I call the 'New Year, New Me' effect. We all know those people who make New Year's resolutions to get in the best shape of their life. The first half of every January is full of these newbies in the gym walking around looking lost. Some of them go straight to the nearest weight machine or treadmill and start to hit it hard on the daily. As a former frequent gym-goer, this used to irk me. I mean, what are these people doing in my space? But the thing I also knew, and that you would start to see, is that around mid to late January, the gym would start to get emptier, returning to pre-new year levels. And the reason is that people would start with the intention of working out hard every day in the expectation of getting quick results. They wanted to hit the gym with intensity to get their version of the perfect body or to get into the best shape of their lives.

But when they don't see results quickly enough, they become disheartened. One day they wake up late, get stuck in the office, or have a birthday party to attend, and they don't have an hour to work out that day. So they miss a day and do nothing. Then one day turns to two, which turns to three, and their momentum stalls.

They then start to say, 'Oh, I've missed too many days this week. Maybe I'll start again next week.'

But next week never comes. And before they know it, they're into February, and they're left with an expensive gym membership to pay for, having signed up for an annual membership because it was cheaper, and they look and feel no different than they did when they first started.

Why?

Because they focused on intensity rather than consistency. They believed that if they didn't have an hour, and they weren't suffering during every minute of that hour, it wasn't worth working out.

The reason this happens is that the focus isn't on achieving a goal they're deeply connected to. The focus isn't on getting to a particular place and becoming a particular person, in a reasonable period of time. The focus is on creating results they think they should be striving for quickly through intensity. They want to do and achieve everything now!

But the thing about an all-or-nothing approach is that, over time, you end up doing nothing. Because maintaining that same level of intensity day in, day out over a long period of time isn't sustainable. It's just not. You can't hit it hard in the gym every day. Your body will break down, you'll get injured, and mentally, you'll get fatigued.

The exact same thing can happen in your career if you're not careful. You'll know it when you're eating dinner at your desk every night or doing all-nighter after all-nighter. It's this time when you're just not thinking straight, when you're just not performing to the best of your ability. Because it's not possible. It's unsustainable. You need time to rest, recharge and recuperate so you can be on your A game. Intuitively it might seem that the more intense you are, the quicker you'll make progress, but intensity only works in short intentional bursts. It's not a sound strategy to sustainably get you to where you want to be in the long term.

So you're probably thinking, *Well, what's the answer here? How do I change that? How do I carve out the time? How do I step back from intensity? What is the answer? Tell me, Ryan!*

Okay, I'm going to stop attacking you about the gym now and go back to Martha's story and how that played out.

So what we did is we explored her story. We explored whether her lack of time story was true or false. And what happened was that as I asked questions, as we worked through the process, and as we continued to explore, what became apparent was that she did have time. Not the multiple hours per day she wanted or thought she needed, but there was some time. There was a pocket of time in the morning before she started work, and when the house was empty. Anywhere from fifteen to thirty minutes. Time that she used to enjoy her morning coffee and typically spent scrolling social media.

And while there's nothing wrong with scrolling social media, what she realised through our coaching conversation was that scrolling social media wasn't supporting her writing dream. It was a realisation that she came to herself: she wanted to be a writer. That was something that excited her, that lit her up more than a mindless scrolling session while waiting for her working day to begin. And once that became apparent, we started to explore what time she would have. It's interesting when I do this with clients, because, again, it comes back to this concept of intensity – people get really excited, and they want to go hard. So they begin by saying, 'Well,

I can commit all of this time. I can commit an hour a day or two hours a day, sometimes more.' And I then have to slowly guide them towards tempering those initial expectations, because again, going back to the gym-goers, all that will happen is you'll commit to an hour a day or two hours a day of, in this instance, writing or reading or taking other steps towards being a writer. But then you'll miss a day or two days, or you won't have an hour or two that day, and you'll tell yourself there's no point doing anything that day as you don't have time. Then before you know it, you've fallen off the wagon, days have passed and you've failed to do the thing you were so excited to do.

It's far better to commit a small amount of time that you know you can easily give on a regular basis. And then if you're in the zone, or you find yourself with more time than expected, just increase the time for that particular session.

So back to Martha, the lawyer who wanted to be a writer. After walking back her initial time commitment from what she thought she should commit to what felt easy to commit, fifteen minutes was where we ended up. A commitment of fifteen minutes a day to her dream of being a writer. And exploring further, she decided that those fifteen minutes didn't have to be spent writing. They could be spent doing anything towards the dream, whether that be reading other writers, researching writing courses, brainstorming ideas, anything. The only requirement was that she treated those fifteen minutes as sacred, as protected time, time solely spent on doing and being the thing she wanted to be and becoming the thing she wanted to become.

Suddenly, it all became so much easier, so much more manageable. And within an hour, she'd gone from feeling overwhelmed and frustrated at there not being enough time to feeling excited about seeing a path to becoming who she wanted to be.

I've done this exercise with clients who want to do or achieve a whole range of things but don't feel they have the time. Clients who want to get back into a consistent workout, clients who want to build a meditation practice, clients who want to build a side hustle or start a training course or master's degree. It's removing the focus on the intensity and reframing it or redirecting it towards consistency. Because it's better to commit fifteen minutes a day, five days a week to becoming a writer than it is to wait for that magical block of time to appear and do nothing.

I always come back to that old Chinese proverb in situations like this: 'The best time to plant a tree was yesterday, the next best time is today.'

The time will pass whatever you do or don't do, so what are you waiting for? How much further along will you be and how much more will you know if you start today with the time you have and remain consistent, rather than waiting for a distant time in the future that may never come, a time when you can spend hours a day getting after the thing you want?

I followed the same process when writing my first book. I couldn't dedicate whole days or multiple hours per day to writing. It just wasn't possible given my circumstances at the time, but I knew I had to write that book. I looked at the easiest amount of time I could commit to and when. It was thirty minutes per day, Monday to Friday, before the kids got up. So I committed to thirty minutes per day. From 5:30 a.m. to 6 a.m., that's when I worked on my book. Some days I'd be in the zone, sit for longer, and write a shit ton of words. Other days, I'd struggle to write a coherent sentence. But committing to thirty minutes, five days per week created a routine, a habit. And it meant that when the alarm went off, there was no question of hitting snooze, much as I wanted to. Because I knew I had to remain consistent in writing. I knew I wouldn't become the author I envisioned and wanted to be if I didn't keep that commitment to myself. That's how the first draft of the book got done in sixty days. When people say, 'Oh, you wrote that book so quickly', that's why. Because I committed to the time I had and focused on consistency rather than intensity.

If I'd waited until I had a chunk of time to write, say six hours every Saturday, I'd still be here today talking about writing a book. As nice as that would be, with all I have going on in life, that time was unlikely to materialise, and even if it did arrive, I wouldn't have built up my confidence and my writing muscle by being consistent, so I wouldn't have written the impactful book I wrote.

So whatever it is you're saying you don't have time for, I want you to ask yourself the following questions:

- ☑ Is this story true?
- ☑ Do I really want to do the thing?
- ☑ Do I really want to live life Lit?
- ☑ Do I really want to explore the ideas, the things I want to do, the things I want to be, the things I want to become?

If you do, you'll find the time – whether it's sitting on the train to the office on your daily commute, getting up thirty minutes before everyone else in your household, or religiously snatching the gaps in your day between calls and meetings.

Step back from the intensity, and focus on the consistency. Focus on taking one small step each day.

Because before you know it, one day you'll look back and be amazed at how far those multiple small steps have taken you.

Some days, that small step will be just that, one small step. You may even think it's so small that it's insignificant. But if you're intentional each day about doing something to move you closer towards your goal, your dream, closer towards living life Lit!, you'll get there a whole lot quicker than if you wait until you feel you have time for a mad sprint of intensity.

So as you finish this chapter, I invite you to think about something you've been thinking of doing but have yet to start.

Got it?

OK, now ask yourself:

What's the smallest step I can take today to make progress towards that thing?

What's an easy amount of time I can spend today on taking that step?

Project Actions

- ☑ Write down something you want to achieve.
- ☑ Allocate a period of time that feels easy to commit to each day to work towards that thing.
- ☑ Schedule that time in your calendar.
- ☑ Set a daily reminder on your phone asking, What's the smallest step I can take today to move closer to my goal?

FINDING CLARITY THROUGH STILLNESS

How many hats do you wear in life?

How many roles do you play?

Without much thought, I can reel off the following roles I play in my life: husband, father, son, brother, uncle, friend, coach, yoga teacher, meditation guide, writer ... phew! I'll stop there.

I invite you to stop reading this book for sixty seconds and list the roles you play. Yeah, I know. I get annoyed when a book tells me to do stuff instead of just letting me passively read then go about my day feeling good about myself and the information I've consumed. Because I know this about myself, I've made it easy for you to make a list by leaving space right here (if you're reading the paperback, that is. If you're reading the e-book, now's the time to click the link and download the workbook.)

OK, did you do it?

How many roles did you list?

I don't know about you, but when I think about all the roles I play and the things I do connected to each role, it feels exhausting. School runs, bathtimes, bedtimes, laundry, cleaning, planning, coaching, teaching, listening, reading, writing, and supporting (emotionally, financially, physically) are just some of the things that come to mind.

And on top of that, each role comes with a certain expectation as to how to perform that role. So not only are you trying to perform the role and do all the things, but you're also trying to do them in the way that others expect you to do them.

So is it any wonder that day-to-day life can leave you feeling frazzled? Even if you're fortunate enough not to be a stressed-out cog in a corporate wheel, you can easily find yourself becoming a stressed-out cog in the parenting wheel or the business wheel or the creative wheel, or simply the wheel of life!

This is what happens when we're always trying to 'do'.

Because, let's face it, there's always something to do, right? Emails to respond to, kids to attend to, friends to connect with, clients to serve, partners to support, taxes to file, ugh!

And although 'doing' makes us feel productive as we cross another thing off a to-do list that never seems to get shorter, only longer, it also places you in a reactionary state, jumping to put out the latest fire, solve the latest problem, or attend to someone else's emergency. It can feel like chaos.

Not the best state for thinking about who you are, what you want, or why you want it. Not the best state for gaining clarity.

See when your mind is constantly running at 100 miles per hour (or 160.93 kilometres per hour for you metric folk), you don't have the space and time to create a vision of the life you want because you're simply trying to get through the day without burning out or breaking down. You're surviving, but by no means thriving.

You know what I'm talking about, right?

I wanted to paint this picture for you so you know that I get it.

I'm not some out-of-touch celebrity lifestyle guru who thinks you have multiple hours each day to luxuriate in bubble baths surrounded by candles, dreaming of the idyllic life you want to live uninterrupted by the demands of kids, a job, and the pressures of everyday life.

This was one of my many frustrations with the world of personal development when I started on my own personal development quest. No one seemed to acknowledge the busyness and messiness of real life for everyday people.

Something that irked me was when one particular 'expert' would wax lyrical about telling your kids, 'Mommy/Daddy is working now so go play quietly until she/he is done' (eye-roll).

As soon as I heard that (and I heard it more than once), I instantly knew that he (of course it was a he) either had the most perfect obedient kids in the world, or he didn't have kids at all. You won't be surprised to know it was the latter.

By the way, if you happen to have kids who listen to what you say and obey your every word, you must let me know what sorcery you practise.

I digress.

Like you, my life is busy.

So when I share the practices I engage in and the habits I've created, I'm showing you them through the real-life lens of a parent of neurodiverse kids, performing multiple roles, while simultaneously trying to maintain my well-being and my relationships and make the vision of the life I want a reality.

So, now we've established all that, let me share with you how I find clarity amidst life's chaos and clear up what on its face may look like a contradiction between the title of this chapter and what I said in my first book.

Now, in *The Triple C Method*®, I said clarity is gained through action, because 'When you take action, everything becomes clearer.' [14]

So you may be wondering why this chapter is titled 'Finding Clarity through Stillness'.

Have I changed my position? Did I lie to you?

---

14 Ryan Spence, *The Triple C Method*® (Sheffield, England, 2022), 50.

Well, the answer to both questions is no!

Although it's fine to change your position once new information comes to light, that isn't what's happened here. Integrity is one of my five core values, so I certainly didn't and wouldn't lie to you. The way I see it, clarity comes through both action and stillness.

I can almost hear the sound of multiple brows furrowing in confusion. But hear me out.

Action moves you forward. And in moving forward you get real-time data about what works for you and what doesn't, what you like and what you don't like.

Take writing a book, for example.

As I've said before, I thought for years about writing a book. I went back and forth about the type of book I wanted to write. Fiction or non-fiction? Did I want to be traditionally published or self-published? How long would it take? Did I have the time? Would anybody care? Did I have anything to say?

So many questions bouncing around in my head.

And you know what happened with all that thinking? Nothing!

No words, no book, no data.

But when I committed to writing a book and began the process of writing, I figured out the answers to all those questions and many more, along the way. Because I was in the process, in motion, I had real-time information

I could act upon. And this action coupled with the data helped me cut through the fog and find clarity on where I wanted to go with the book I was writing and prevented my wayward thoughts from taking the wheel and spinning me out like a boy-racer in a pimped-out ride doing doughnuts in an empty parking lot.

So I stick by what I said in *The Triple C Method*®: action leads to clarity.

But, as I mentioned earlier in this chapter, when you're constantly on the go and busy 'doing', your mind is like the spin cycle on a washing machine, whizzing around with a jumble of ideas, solutions, problems and issues as you react to all that's going on around you rather than calmly addressing each situation with intention.

That's where stillness comes in.

Stillness gives you the space and time to pause, to breathe, to detach from the noise and clear the windscreen of your mind. It allows you to see your thoughts while at the same time recognising that you are not your thoughts, so you don't need to cling on to them for dear life. You can let go.

Imagine you're sitting on a park bench meditating. Your eyes are open as you stare into the distance, your diffused vision softening your focus. In your peripheral vision, you notice a bird flying in from your right. You see it as it crosses your line of vision and you acknowledge its existence, its beauty, its magnificence. But as it continues to fly off to your left, you don't turn your head to follow it. You remain staring at the vision in front of you or focused on the anchor of your meditation, as the bird slowly disappears from view. You're not following the bird's flight. You're noticing it's there, acknowledging its existence but allowing it to pass without attachment. You're not dwelling on what type of bird it is, what it looks like, where it's going, what it's doing, or what it's thinking. You're simply thinking, *Oh, there's a bird*, and then letting all thought of the bird go.

That's what it means to sit in stillness and detach from your thoughts. That's what it means to meditate.

Now, before you switch off and say,

Oh, I can't meditate.

Meditation's not for me. I tried it once and I couldn't sit still.

My mind's too busy to meditate.

Stay with me. Keep an open mind. Relax, listen in.

I used to be exactly the same!

My road to meditation was filled with frustration, false starts, and the belief that it was only for Buddhist monks sitting in hilltop caves isolated from the outside world, not busy people like me. But as I came to realise, if you think you're too busy to meditate, you're exactly the person who needs to meditate.

I was introduced to meditation when I began practising yoga many, many years ago. I talk more about my yoga journey in chapter 5 of this book, but for the purpose of this chapter, my initial reason for practising was to counter my limited flexibility and mobility, as a result of regularly playing football and failing to properly stretch! I was as stiff as the Tin Man, the least flexible person in the room, often the only guy, and the only Black person in class. Suffice to say, I felt a little out of place. But every time I finished class, I felt a sense of peace in a way I never had before. So I kept going to class off and on for years.

Although initially I went for the physical movement, the more I practised the more I found I loved the stillness at the start and end of class and the way it settled my monkey mind. So I began to try to introduce stillness to my life outside of class and off the mat. I wanted to recreate that sense of calm, peace, and inner connection on a more consistent basis, without having to rely on attending a yoga class to get it.

Even though I was now open to meditating, I still found it hard to connect to the process and build a consistent practice without the guidance of an in-person teacher. As a hip-hop-loving Black guy from a council estate in

England who often felt like a fish out of water in a yoga class, it was hard for me to marry this persona with the practice of meditation and the identity of a meditator. I liked being alone, but I was so conditioned to always be doing something, to be productive, that the stillness and quiet made me restless.

Meditation really clicked for me when I read the book *Success Through Stillness* by Russell Simmons and Chris Morrow. Russell Simmons, along with famed music producer Rick Rubin, founded the iconic hip-hop record label Def Jam Recordings If you're into hip-hop, you know about Def Jam, and if you're not, you've likely heard of some Def Jam artists like LL Cool J, Run DMC and the late great DMX. For a long time, in the 1980s and early 1990s, Russell was hip-hop. He was also a party guy, a successful entrepreneur, and someone who preached the virtue of hustling hard.

For someone like me, from my background, Russell Simmons was a relatable example of someone who, to paraphrase the rapper Drake, started from the bottom and now he's here.

So hearing that through yoga and meditation Russell had turned his life around was intriguing. If he had done it, with his background and lifestyle, maybe there was something in it for me too.

That book was instrumental in making me a meditation convert and it's a book I've shared with friends, colleagues and clients interested in, but sceptical about, meditation. It also probably, subconsciously, played a part in my becoming vegan several years later. The beauty of the book is in its simplicity – in the way it demystifies what meditation is, breaks down why meditation is for everybody, and extolls the many benefits of this ancient yogic practice.

If you're still reading, I'm going to guess that you're at least curious about meditation. And that's good. Follow that curiosity.

There's this belief that in order to be a 'good meditator' (there is no such thing by the way), you have to sit with an empty mind, devoid of all thoughts, or enter a state of hypnosis and completely forget who or where you are as you get lost in some mystical trance.

None of that is true. Everyday people meditate. People you've seen on the street, people you work with, people just like you with stressful jobs, busy lives, and big dreams, they meditate. Lawyers, doctors, nurses, accountants, athletes – meditators can be found in pretty much every walk of life if you look hard enough.

Meditation isn't something that's just for people who go on retreats or hang out in mountainside caves or backpack around India to find themselves. It's for everybody. It's been around for thousands of years, and it works by giving you the space and time to just be and not do, to enter stillness so you can listen to what your mind, body and breath are telling you. It allows you to connect with your inner knowing so you can find the answers to the questions you;ve been asking about your life.

'But Ryan,' you cry, 'I'm far too busy to meditate.'

I used to say the same and here's what I learned.

You may have heard the Zen proverb 'You should sit in meditation for twenty minutes every day, unless you're too busy, then you should sit for an hour.'

I used to find this so annoying!

My thought was always that I'm a busy and important BigLaw lawyer, so finding twenty minutes a day to 'navel-gaze' (yeah, that's what I thought about this ancient practice, I'm now embarrassed to admit) seemed ridiculous to me. I mean, sitting still for five minutes was difficult enough. It's unproductive and not conducive to achieving success in our productivity-driven world. I have:

- ☑ emails to reply to,
- ☑ documents to review, and
- ☑ billable hours targets to hit.

So with all those demands and all that chaos going on around me, how the hell can sitting in stillness help?

But once I got over myself, kept attending yoga classes, read Russell's book, and opened my mind, I got it. Sitting in stillness became easier. Not easy, but easier.

And I found that in that stillness,

- ☑ time slowed down,
- ☑ my stress and anxiety subsided, and
- ☑ I gained a clarity of thought that I hadn't experienced in a long time.

And the more I sat, the more meditation became a necessary support to my well-being. It wasn't all plain sailing though. Old habits, thoughts and beliefs die hard, so I would find myself falling off the meditation wagon from time to time. When I didn't meditate, I noticed the anxiety creeping back in, the stress levels rising, and my intentionality waning. I would notice myself reacting in ways I didn't want to and getting attached to situations and things that didn't serve me. But as I'd built a base level of self-awareness, I knew what was missing, so I'd get back on track and consciously make the effort to reconnect with myself so I could regain the clarity I'd lost.

The more I saw and felt a greater sense of clarity, a deeper sense of self, a stronger connection to my intuition, and an ability to detach from situations and outcomes and remain focused on the bigger picture, the deeper my Why for meditating became. So I kept coming back to it. And now I can't imagine my life without meditation in it.

Has my story deepened your curiosity?

OK, great!

Because I'm going to share with you how you can get started on your meditation journey even if you think you're the busiest, most restless person in the world.

Starting Your Practice

The excellent news is that despite what the aforementioned proverb says you don't need to start with twenty minutes.

Even focusing on your breath for sixty seconds before responding to that snarky email from the lawyer on the other side of that horrendous soul-sucking deal will allow you to detach from what you think and respond to what is.

You don't have to sit cross-legged or in the lotus position.

You don't need any fancy props.

Just find a quiet place where you won't be disturbed, then sit, breathe, and be.

It's simple, but not easy. And you're going to encounter discomfort, both physical and mental, as you fight against the long-conditioned urge to be doing something, to be productive, to be taking action.

Don't fight it. Allow it. Notice what comes up. This is the practice.

Remember, all you're doing here is being a human being, instead of a human doing.

And if you keep going and build up consistency in your practice, in time you'll find that in simply being, you'll start to gain more clarity. So when you do take action, those actions will be from a place of intention not reaction.

To return to something I said earlier in this chapter, when you're always on the go, always moving at 100 miles an hour, it's hard to get a handle on your thoughts and explore what they really mean, so you tell yourself stories about what you think they mean. It's hard for the truth in those thoughts to shine through because your parasympathetic nervous system is jacked up and you're constantly living in a heightened state of alertness, running on to the next situation, emergency, or crisis, to avoid the discomfort of being alone with yourself and your thoughts.

But allowing yourself that space on a daily basis to just *be* trains your mind to search for and find that space beyond your meditation practice, to find space within your daily routine and activities. So that when something 'bad' or annoying happens, like your boss is micromanaging you to the state of annoyance, instead of reacting in the heat of the moment and telling them what you really think, you'll have trained yourself to take a breath, tap into the skill that you've built, and detach from the situation so you can respond from a place of intention, not reaction.

When someone cuts you off in traffic, and you feel that road rage boiling up inside of you, your meditation practice will allow you to recognise the rage, detach from the situation, and see it's not worth your time as it doesn't serve you and your mission to allow that rage to boil over.

This doesn't mean you're going to be perfect; you're human after all. I still get mad; I still get angry. But the difference is that the anger is now more often than not proportional to whatever it is that has happened. And I have the time and space to look at the situation differently, asking myself what do I want to do here? What do I need to do to move forward in a way that serves me?

I've broken this down into a simple three-part process I follow when shit happens and I'm going to share it with you here.

It's my Triple A Process. Yep, three letters again.

Acknowledge, Accept, Adapt.

This process was borne out of my meditation practice, and it's a process I share with my coaching clients when they're dealing with a difficult situation. When something happens that annoys you, that makes you angry or frustrated, and your instinct is to react from that state in a way that doesn't serve you or your purpose, here's how you use the process. You stop, focus on your breath, then:

Acknowledge: Acknowledge what is happening or what has happened. Don't brush it under the carpet or practise toxic positivity. If it's shit, it's shit. Acknowledge that.

Accept: Accept what's happened. Wishing it hadn't happened is normal, but it's also unhelpful as you can't change it, so get yourself to a place of acceptance. How long this takes will depend on the severity of the situation and how it's affected you.

Adapt: What are you going to do with this new situation you find yourself in? You can let it stop you moving forward or you can adapt your strategy and change course to account for the challenge or obstacle.

I walked Alyssia, a former client of mine, through this process when she had a career setback. One of her goals at the start of our work together was to secure a new job. She felt stuck in a rut in her current position at an organisation she'd worked at for more than 10 years and was struggling to find a new role, partly because she lacked clarity on what she wanted the next stage of her career and her life to look like. By the end of our time working together, and after gaining the clarity she previously lacked, she applied for and got a new role. Unfortunately, shortly after starting it became apparent that the role wasn't all she had been led to believe it would be. She felt angry, frustrated and deflated and I could see she was in danger of falling back into the rut she'd worked so hard to escape. So, the first thing I asked her to do was to acknowledge the situation and how she felt about it. Acknowledge that she'd left a longstanding position to take on a role that ultimately wasn't right for her, she was angry and frustrated about that. Then take as much time as necessary to sit with those feelings.

Once she had acknowledged and felt all the feels, I invited her to accept the situation as it was, not as she wished it to be. It was clear the role and the organisation wasn't going to change so holding on in the hope that it would and putting a positive spin on everything wasn't going to be helpful here, it would simply delay the inevitable descent into rut she'd escaped from. So, she had to get to a place of acceptance, a place where she could admit to herself it wasn't working, it was never going to work, and she had to intentionally do something to change her situation.

Finally, once she got to the place of acceptance, it was time for her to adapt. This stage was all about reconnecting with the vision of the life she wanted and creating space to think strategically about her options. It involved going a back over work we had previously done together on the 3Cs, finding another layer of clarity, revisiting past experience to build the body of evidence necessary to boost her confidence, and using courage stacking to build the courage to let people know about her situation and boldly ask for help.

At the time of writing she's now sitting on a couple of new job offers and has a killer idea for a side hustle building on skills and talents she already has. That's the power of this Triple A Process.

There's no set timeframe for working through this process. Alyssia worked through all three stages in around four weeks but every situation is different and every situation hits each person with a different level of intensity. The harder a particular situation hits you, the longer it may take you to work through each stage.

For the Triple A Process to really work, you have to be prepared to take the time to build a meditation practice that works for you and that you'll maintain over time. After all, consistency beats intensity, right?

To help you, I've recorded a short meditation that you can access for free in the workbook, so if you haven't downloaded it yet (seriously, what are you waiting for?), now's a good time to do so. Whether you're new to meditation or have dabbled from time to time, try it out and see what changes for you as you take time each day to sit in stillness and connect with your mind, body and breath and find clarity through the stillness.

Project Actions

- ☑ Commit to meditating for two minutes daily.
- ☑ Schedule your meditation time.
- ☑ Keep a meditation journal to capture your pre and post meditation reflections.

IT'S NOT ABOUT SHAPES; IT'S ABOUT SELF

There's a common misconception that yoga is for the few.

That it's a practice only for beautiful babes in bikinis in Bali or hench hunks in high-rise shorts in Hispaniola.[15]

I believe this is a crying shame as both a yoga teacher and someone whose life is infinitely better because of yoga. And it's simply not true!

I understand why the misconception arises. You only have to search 'yoga' on social media or Google to find a myriad of images that support the prevailing stereotype. But by accepting the stereotypical yoga influencer view of what it means to be a yoga practitioner, you lose out on what yoga can give you, the stressed-out lawyer, burnt-out corporate cog, or pissed-off parent.

---

15 OK, I've never seen anyone doing yoga in Hispaniola, but I'm a sucker for alliteration. And when you search Google for a tropical island that begins with H, this is what comes up, so ...

And take it from someone who knows: yoga can give you a lot if you open your heart and mind and let it.

What yoga means to me has evolved since I first stepped on a mat more than twenty years ago as a seven-year-old boy.[16]

I remember taking my first class at Triyoga in Primrose Hill, London. This was around the time yoga was still seen as something only women did (which is strange seeing as, historically, yoga was taught by men and practised by young boys), but a handful of male footballers had outed themselves as avid yoga-goers and were extolling its virtues in aiding their post-match recovery.

And that's why I went.

I wasn't a professional footballer, but I was a keen amateur. In fact I was my university football team's lead striker and top scorer for four seasons straight![17]

Anyway, I digress.

At the time, yoga seemed expensive to me, coming in at £11 for a single drop-in class.[18] I was working full-time in retail at a mobile phone shop, studying law part-time at university, and living in an amazing flat owned by

---

16 OK, there's one untruth in this entire book and this might be it!

17 It's my book and I'll brag if I want to.

18 A price that hasn't changed much today.

a friend in Camden, North London, that was a stretch to afford even on mate's rates, so I wasn't exactly rolling in cash.

But I wanted the physical benefits I kept hearing yoga could provide. I wanted to be able to touch my toes, sit cross-legged on the grass in the park on a summer's day and reduce the muscle pulls and strains common to your average amateur footballer and gym rat. So I scraped together the money to join a class, and one warm summer evening, I made the ten-minute walk from my flat along the canal and through the park to try this yoga thing.

As the studio started to fill with people, I noticed I was the only guy and non-White person in the room. Then, as we were invited to sit cross-legged on our mats, I scanned the room and realised I was the only one who couldn't do it! I was as stiff as the Tin Man from *The Wizard of Oz*; my legs didn't move that way. We'd barely moved and I was already sweating uncomfortably, questioning why the hell I'd thought this would be a good idea. And as the rest of the class effortlessly flowed through the sequence, I became increasingly annoyed and frustrated as my body simply refused to do what I wanted it to do.

With each change in pose, I heard my body telling my brain, *I don't think so, homie*, as it cackled maniacally.

I got cramp in places I never knew you could get cramp, and I huffed and puffed as I clumsily moved from pose to pose, always seeming to be a few beats behind the rest of the class.

To say the class was a struggle would be an understatement. But I stuck with it, and by the end of class, I noticed a difference in myself. A sense of calm and inner peace like I'd never felt before washed over my sweaty, achy body and perpetually busy mind. And this feeling continued as I walked, no floated, from the yoga studio back to my flat, knowing that one day I'd be back.

Whenever I could cobble enough cash together, I'd head to Triyoga to put myself through the physical discomfort, craving the mental clarity and sense of achievement I'd be rewarded with at the end of class.

Eventually, the pressures of time and money meant I had to take time away from the studio and my practice. I occasionally tried to practise at home, but I hadn't yet developed the discipline to consistently cultivate a home practice.

So my practice remained dormant until I entered the world of BigLaw.

Yoga helped me immensely as a BigLaw lawyer. If you've been in that world or a world like it, you'll know the stress, anxiety, and burnout that occur from an always-on culture that rewards those who are willing to sacrifice everything and put the organisation first.

And in that environment, my practice became a lifeline. Now that I had the money I'd previously lacked, yoga stopped being a choice and became a necessity as I attempted to navigate my way through, and find my place in, a world that was alien to me so I could meet and fulfil the definition of success we're conditioned to buy into.

As my practice deepened, I began to realise there was more to yoga than trying to contort my body into shapes it had no business being in. My practice took on greater meaning and impacted my life in ways I never imagined it would back when I first stepped on a yoga mat. The physical movement, the asana, is the entry point, the gateway, to the practice of yoga. But yoga is so much more than you see in an influencer's handstand in a tropical location captioned with the hashtag 'Good Vibes Only'.

So, if you've written off yoga because you're not flexible or you can't do a headstand or handstand, if you've dismissed yoga as something other people do and put yourself in a box marked 'Yoga's not for me', I want to share some of what it means and invite you to step out of that box for a moment to embark on this practice that will help you find your peace.

Yoga is about self-discovery. It's, the journey of the self, through the self, to the self.[19]

When you step on the mat and flow through a sequence you may have done many times before, it's in the repetition, the familiarity of the sequence, that you discover who you are and where you are at any given moment. And where and who you are today may not be the same as where or who you were yesterday or where or who you'll be tomorrow.

The aim of the practice is not to allow the repetition to become habitual, as if you're running on autopilot, but to enter each pose and flow through every transition with intention noticing what comes up for you. How do you feel in your body? What's going on in your mind?

When you step on the mat and are met with a new sequence and new poses, it's in the process of challenging yourself to enter those poses physically and mentally that you discover who you are. Are you resistant to change and judgmental about your abilities and where you think you should be? Or are you open to new challenges and opportunities and accepting of where

---

19 This quote is attributed to the ancient Hindu scripture *The Bhagavad Gita*, required reading in all yoga teacher trainings. The quote itself does not appear in a specific chapter and verse and may not be a direct translation of the original text but rather a modern interpretation of a particular theme contained in the scripture.

you are in that moment? The pose isn't the goal of the practice; it's what you learn and who you become in the process of working towards that pose.

Whatever's happening in life will be revealed on the mat. And whatever you learn on the mat can help you in life. Do you tend to avoid difficult situations in life? This will show up on the mat when you prioritise comfort over challenge – when, for example, your teacher invites you to hold your body in chair pose for ten breaths and you immediately decide it's too hard, you can't do it, so you quit. But as you continue to practise and become more connected with your mind, body and breath, you'll become curious as to how you react to challenges and why you react that way, and you'll become intentional as to how you want to approach them instead.

Yoga makes you confront what's going on. If you practise with intention, follow the sequence, and don't skip the hard parts just because they're hard, you'll begin to notice where you're feeling:

- ☑ resistance,
- ☑ fearful,
- ☑ anxious,
- ☑ contentment,
- ☑ anger, or
- ☑ joy.

It all comes out on the mat. It all comes out in yoga.

Yoga will deliver your truth, whether you like it or not, no matter how much you try to hide it. It's up to you to listen and decide what to do with it.

Yoga teacher and author Richard Freeman says, 'Yoga begins with listening. When we listen, we are giving space to what it is.'[20]

So I invite you to step onto your mat and start listening. Listen to your mind, your body, your breath, and that inner knowing that resides deep within your soul. What you hear may just surprise you and provide you with some of the answers to life's questions that you've been looking for.

I know starting something new can be hard. And, as I shared in this chapter, I know it can be daunting to step into a yoga studio as a newbie. So to help you get started on discovering what yoga can do for you, I'm giving you access to my Flow in Fifteen sequence, a simple fifteen-minute practice to get you moving on your mat and guide you back to yourself. This practice, filmed in a beautiful space in Singapore, is something I've previously shared with my 1:1 coaching clients to help kickstart their practice. And before you start

---

[20] Richard Freeman, The Mirror of Yoga (Boston, Massachusetts), ix.

listening to that part of your brain telling you, *I don't have time to do this*, that's exactly why it's only fifteen minutes. Because whatever else is going on in your life right now, I know you have fifteen minutes to focus on your well-being. If you don't, I direct you back to chapter 3 of this book.

Links to the video and accompanying guidebook can be found in, you guessed it, the workbook (you have downloaded it now, right?).

Project Actions

- ☑ Commit to 30 days of yoga.
- ☑ Schedule your yoga time in your calendar.
- ☑ Keep a yoga journal to record any mental, physical and emotional shifts you notice.

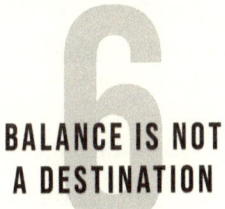

BALANCE IS NOT A DESTINATION

We were on a family holiday in the northern seaside town of Filey, North Yorkshire, England. After an incident on the beach involving the youngest child wandering off to pick blackberries, completely oblivious to the mayhem and panic he left behind as everyone searched for him, we relocated to the safer confines of a playground for a well-earned rest. The plan was that the parents would sit on a bench resting and recuperating while the kids would run around in the sun expending every last bit of pent-up energy ready for what we hoped would be an early bedtime (wishful thinking).

That isn't quite how it all played out.

Interspersed between the two boys alternating between playing together and trying to kill each other were frequent requests to push them on the swings, throw them in the air, and perform the role of a monster chasing them around the park. So much for some R 'n R.

Then at some point, they headed towards the big red and yellow see-saw and insisted my wife and I come along with them.

At this time, my kids were aged six and four. And when they sat on each end of the see-saw, the weight was unbalanced as you'd expect, with the four-year-old sitting slightly higher in the air. He asked me to come and sit with him. So I walked over, pulled down his side of the see-saw, and climbed aboard.

What do you think happened next?

Well, of course, me being an adult, a vegan athlete no less, the weight shifted so that now my six-year-old was high up in the air while my four-year-old and I were rooted to the ground.

So then the six-year-old roped my wife in and she climbed onto his side of the see-saw. That shifted the balance a little, but the see-saw still wasn't fully balanced. We played around with this for a while, changing the configuration of humans on each end of the see-saw but we never found the perfect balance. It simply didn't exist.

What we did find was joy and laughter no matter where we were on the see-saw. We didn't give up playing on the see-saw; we kept enjoying the process of trying to find balance.

I share this because it's a great metaphor for life. Many talk about striving for balance, in particular work-life balance, as if balance is a thing to be found, a destination to be reached.

Yet if we're expecting to find the perfect ratio between all of life's demands that bring us to equilibrium, the only thing we can expect to find is disappointment. Because life is never balanced.

We never have everything fully in check, or fully where we want it to be.

Sometimes some things are up, some things are down. And sometimes you'll have that occasional moment, that scintilla of time, where everything feels perfectly aligned. Like the old saying 'Even a stopped clock is right two times a day', even a see-saw is balanced at some point as the weight distribution shifts, even if only for a millisecond when one side comes down as the other flies up.

But as soon as you find that micromoment of balance, something happens to knock you off course and you're right back where you started, beating yourself up for never, in your eyes, quite having it all together. I get it. We all want to be great parents, friends, partners, spouses, employees, and leaders, and when we feel we're lacking in any of those areas, it's human nature to question our competence, our value, our worth.

But where does that get you? For me, it got me deep in the depths of self-flagellation and self-loathing and, in my darkest moments, questioning the point of my very existence. I mean, if I couldn't do everything perfectly, in the way we're conditioned to believe they're supposed to be done, what was even the point in trying anymore?

But through coaching, I realised thinking that way does you a disservice. It places an unrealistic expectation on you to be this perfectly balanced, perfectly aligned human being that never fucks up and never drops the ball.

And that's just not realistic.

I don't believe it ever was, but it especially isn't realistic in today's world. The demands on our time keep increasing. And the technology that was supposed to save us, to buy us back our time and freedom, instead consumes our every waking hour, by:

- ☑ luring us into doomscrolling our social media feeds;
- ☑ bombarding us with more information than our brains are designed to handle, information that often leaves us feeling even more shit and inadequate about the lack of balance in our lives; and
- ☑ keeping us permanently connected to our jobs whether we're at dinner, on holiday, or asleep.

So what does that mean? Does that mean that we should ignore balance completely and throw our hands in the air as we resign ourselves to accepting defeat because we're all flawed human beings who can't get anything right?

This may be a controversial answer but, well, yes. I believe we should accept our flaws, embrace them even. Rather than fall into the bottomless pit of compare and despair, we'd be a whole lot happier and healthier if we embraced our uniqueness. But just because you accept that you're flawed, it doesn't mean you give up on life.

The quest for balance is a noble one and one I believe we should pursue. It builds character and resilience and expands your capacity as to what you believe you can achieve. But the key thing to remember is that balance isn't a destination. And by that I mean you don't put your life on hold waiting to enjoy it once you arrive at the perfect balance. You don't spend day after day beating yourself up for dropping one ball here and one ball there.

No!

The pursuit of balance should be enjoyed, not endured. Much like moving up and down on a see-saw.

As the four of us sat on that see-saw, we knew we were never going to achieve the perfect balance. It's simple physics. We'd need equal weight at the perfect time and that was never going to happen. But there was still joy in trying; there was still joy in the process. My kids still squealed with delight as they moved up and down amidst shouts of, 'Again! Again!' Isn't that the point of a see-saw? Isn't that the point of life?

You can get so fixated on the pursuit of work-life balance and how you're failing to get anywhere close to it. Haranguing yourself for not leaving the office in time to make it home for dinner, missing your child's nativity play because someone stuck a meeting in your calendar, cancelling dinner with your friends for the umpteenth time because you got stuck with an urgent deadline just as you were about to head out the door.

But the great thing about feeling and thinking all these things is that you've reached the first step in changing your life from one where you're surviving to one where you're thriving: awareness. You've realised you're on the see-saw and, unlike my kids, you're not enjoying the ride.

Congratulations! You're already further ahead in the journey back to yourself than many of your peers.

In that awareness, you begin to notice the areas of your life you've neglected. The parts of you that are floating around and only given attention once you've committed to external demands and expectations that don't align with your values and don't serve your life's purpose.

Now you have that awareness you can start to make decisions from a place of intention. To do that, start by asking yourself:

What am I neglecting that's important to me?

Why am I neglecting it? Is it because it's not a priority now or is it because I'm allowing things that aren't a priority to overshadow it?

Where am I in my life right now? Am I at a place where it's ok to focus more on A, knowing and accepting that I'll be out of balance with B, C and maybe D right now?

Or to be more specific:

Am I at a stage where putting my work and career first serves me even though doing so may impact my well-being and relationships in the short to medium term?

These questions will help deepen your awareness. And as long as you carry that awareness with you daily and continue being curious as to why your life is the way it is and whether you want it to be that way, that's where you'll find the answers you're looking for.

Maybe you're going through a particularly busy period at work, and you haven't spent as much time with your kids, partner, or friends as you'd like. As long as you recognise that early, intentionally decide that this is the right thing for you to do right now, are clear as to why that's the case, and make a plan to switch your attention and focus on redressing that balance when that busy period is over, you'll glide smoothly on the seesaw. What you don't want is to wake up six months, one year, three years from now feeling just as busy, being just as neglectful, and wondering where your life went.

All this really comes down to is being clear and intentional about where you're spending your time and why and looking for those moments when it's appropriate to start to redress the balance.

What I don't want you to do and what isn't productive is using the lack of balance you feel you have in your life as a stick to beat yourself with.

I haven't spent enough time with my kids today. I'm a bad parent.

I should have stayed at work longer and finished that email. I'm a bad employee.

I haven't been to the gym today. I can't stick to anything.

Stop beating yourself up!

Instead, come back to your values. Come back to what's important to you. And then look at where you're out of alignment and figure out why.

Are you carrying too heavy a load in a particular area? What can you do to shed some of that?

Are people sitting on your see-saw who don't need to be there and are only weighing you down? How do you want to deal with that?

And above all else, accept that balance is an illusion as it pertains to life. You will fall out of alignment. Things will come up to destroy your best-laid plans. You may even get knocked off your see-saw sometimes. But the key is to be aware when all of this is happening so you can recognise the cause and take intentional steps to deal with it.

Now, I know you're thinking, *How the hell do I get started?*

And, as always, I've got you. Here's a simple exercise to get you rocking that see-saw with the wild abandon of a four-year-old child.

The Daily Check-In

At the end of each day, check in with yourself.

Look at your core values[21] and ask yourself these questions:

- ☑ *Where did I live my values today?*
- ☑ *Where was I out of alignment?*
- ☑ *What's one thing I can commit to doing tomorrow to realign with my values?*[22]

That's it.

Over time you'll become a master at noticing when that see-saw is tipping too far in a particular direction. You'll notice the situations, events, and triggers that always tip you out of alignment. And when you notice, you'll be able to make the changes you need to make, the changes that serve who you want to be and where you want to go. Enjoy the process, and have fun with it. That's the ebb and flow of life.

---

[21] If you don't know what your core values are, I invite you to do the Values exercise in the workbook for my last book, *The Triple C Method®*. You can download that workbook at: iamryanspence.com/the-triple-c-method-book.

[22] You can also find these questions in the workbook accompanying this book. Get it at iamryanspence.com/project

Project Actions

- ☑ Write down your five core values and stick them somewhere you can see them every day.
- ☑ Do a daily check-in for the next 30 days.

OVERCOMING OVERWHELM

What do you do when you feel overwhelmed? When the emails won't stop flooding your inbox. When the phone won't stop ringing. When your boss excitedly bursts into your office with news of yet another deal, and you sit behind your desk wearing a fake smile while mentally calculating the many long-standing commitments you'll now be expected to cancel to complete this new addition to your already excessive workload.

Maybe you scream. Maybe you shout. Maybe you rant to your office mate, who truly understands your plight. Maybe you stress-eat a family-sized bag of tortilla chips (lightly salted Doritos for me). Maybe you chug a glass of wine to take the edge off the day (a full-bodied red was my weapon of choice).

But after the day you've had, you know one glass (even a large glass) just isn't going to cut it. The way you're feeling requires a hell of a lot more than that to numb the pain. Glass one is gone in sixty seconds. You feel that familiar buzz as the alcohol hits your system, then you pour yourself a second. And as you reach the bottom of the glass, feeling a little warm, a little light-headed, but a whole lot better than when you started, you think, *Fuck it, I've started, so I may as well finish.* And before you know it you've woken up sprawled on the sofa feeling groggy, disorientated, with some show you don't care about blasting out from the TV, empty glass in hand and empty bottle on the table.

All of the above are understandable responses to feeling out of control. Feeling your life is not your own. But when you've eaten the chips and finished the wine, what's next? Do you tell yourself, 'It is what it is', and resign yourself to a lifetime of being stuck in the fog of anger, frustration and lethargy? Do you accept this cycle will continue to replay itself and there's nothing you can do to change that?

Or do you draw a line in the sand, say, 'Enough is enough', and rather than passively accept your situation, actively explore ways to escape, ways to break the cycle of destructive acts that exacerbate your feelings of helplessness, leaving you feeling unmotivated and disengaged, like an extra in your life instead of the leading star?

Now, I'm in no way judging you. I won't be telling you to be grateful for what you have, suck it up and keep it moving.

I won't do that because I've been there, stress-eating the Doritos and knocking back the Rioja. And I know from my own experience that this kind of talk is neither helpful nor productive.

I also know that the actions you take are not your fault. You're in a battle against an enemy you're unaware of. An enemy you can't see. An enemy so pervasive, persistent and persuasive that it leaves you constantly feeling like a failure. Who or what is this enemy?

The enemy is overwhelm.

Overwhelm is a sneaky motherfucker. One minute you feel fine, busy but able to deal with the copious amount of shit on your plate; you're keeping calm and carrying on while multiple fires blaze around you. Then, boom! Overwhelm swaggers up to you with a glint in its eye and hits you square in the face like a lightning fast jab from a heavyweight boxer.

Overwhelm crushes your spirit and attempts to break your soul.

The process feels like when you go out for a long run. You start the run feeling fresh and ready to slay, telling yourself, 'I got this', as you glide through the streets like a professional athlete (in your mind at least). Then, over time your legs begin to feel heavy, sluggishness sets in, and your inner critic cajoles you into giving up because it's all too much, too hard, and you don't need to be doing this. You keep pushing, telling yourself that if you just keep doing the same thing you've been doing, you'll be fine. But now each step feels like you're wading through quicksand, and suddenly you stop, unable to run, walk, or stagger a step further.

That's what overwhelm feels like. The sluggishness, the heaviness, the rattling of the naysayer voice in your head.

But the good news is you're stronger than overwhelm and you can fight back. The most effective weapon I've found to keep overwhelm at bay and make it STFU is stillness.

I talked about stillness in chapter 4 as it relates to meditation, so why am I mentioning it again now? Because the power of a stillness practice cannot be underestimated. So, if you can't quite get your head around the idea of meditating just yet, start taking time in your day to simply be still.

Seventeenth-century French philosopher Blaise Pascal said, 'All of humanity's problems stem from man's inability to sit quietly in a room alone.'[23] And in my view he was right.

For overwhelm to thrive, it needs you to be constantly doing, trying to do all the things and worrying you won't get them all done on time or perfectly. So detaching yourself from multiple situations, sitting still, alone in a room, focusing on one thing is kryptonite to overwhelm. It doesn't matter what you focus on. It could be the beating of your pulse in your fingertips, the sensation of the air on your skin, or the spot on the wall before you. For me, the easiest thing to focus on is my breath. The breath is powerful, and the correct technique can simulate your vagus nerve, resetting your central nervous system and returning you to a calm, relaxed state where overwhelm struggles to survive.

Now, don't get it twisted. This isn't where this book turns into some toxic positivity bullshit and I tell you to sit quietly, think happy thoughts, and everything will be fine.

Hell no! We don't do that over here. Sometimes things are fucked and we have to sit with that.

---

23 Oliver Burkeman, 'This Column Will Change Your Life: Just Sit down and Think', *The Guardian*, 2014 https://www.theguardian.com/lifeandstyle/2014/jul/19/change-your-life-sit-down-and-think, accessed 9 July 2024.

The point of being still here isn't to think positively; it's to think, well, nothing. It's to recognise your thoughts but also as I said before, to recognise your thoughts are not you. Overwhelm is not you.

Of course, thoughts will arise; a clear, blank slate of a mind isn't the goal here.

But when thoughts do appear, all you need to do is watch them flicker through your mind, like a movie or TV show. You know when you mindlessly binge the latest trending Netflix show after another day of overwhelm kicking your ass? That's exactly how you watch your thoughts in stillness.

See, the thing about overwhelm is it hates you being still because it needs your frantic helpless energy to thrive. It feeds off your stress and anxiety. It loves when you constantly run on a hamster wheel, trying to keep up with the demands of life, and trying to measure up to the incessant societal expectation to be useful and productive as if your only value to the world is how much you can produce and how much money you can make for people and organisations that, frankly, don't need any more.

So the way to fight overwhelm is to refuse to feed it.

Refuse to allow yourself to be hurried, harried and hustled.

Refuse to live your life in a perpetual state of motion.

Refuse to wear busyness as a badge of honour.

Instead, choose stillness because overwhelm hates stillness.

Overwhelm is no pushover. It will put up a good fight, bombarding you with thoughts about all the things you absolutely must do, all the places you absolutely must be, all the actions you absolutely must take.

At first, it will whisper to you in seductive tones:

Just do this thing,

Imagine the praise you'll get if you tick all these things off your list today.

You don't need to take a break, just keep pushing.

Then, as you get stronger, more aware, and better at not succumbing to its charms, it will change tack and scream at you:

WHAT ARE YOU DOING? WE DON'T HAVE TIME TO SIT STILL!

WE HAVE EMAILS TO READ, MEETINGS TO ATTEND, DOCUMENTS TO DRAFT!

WHO'S GOING TO DO ALL THAT IF YOU'RE SITTING ON YOUR ASS BEING STILL?!

And when that happens. When overwhelm loses its cool and flies into a rage, you know you've got to it. And now you're under its skin; ignore it. You're in control here. You choose what to do, when to do it, and how.

You don't have to let overwhelm guilt-trip you into doing it all now. You don't have to let overwhelm guilt-trip you into doing anything.

Stillness allows you to recognise this. It allows you to regain control and fight back against the runaway freight train of overwhelm. But it's a practice. The first few times you sit, it will seem an impossible task. You'll grab on to every thought, dwell on it, ruminate on it, stress over it, and feel the constant urge to get back to doing, back to busyness, back to action, all so you don't have to deal with the discomfort of overwhelm's voice in your head and what's happening within.

I urge you, though, not to give in. Start small and keep at it.

Take the lesson from chapter 3 and start with what feels easy to commit to. Five minutes, one minute, hell even thirty seconds if that's all you can stand right now. Just do it. Find moments of stillness. Every. Single. Day.

The shifts will be subtle, but I promise you, there will be shifts.

You'll begin to notice that when overwhelm appears, and it will still appear, it doesn't hang around for long because now you've robbed it of its power.

It can't stand that you now have the strength to resist its overtures. It can't stand that you've discovered its arch nemesis, stillness. It can't stand that instead of dancing frantically to its tune, you can now be still and listen to your tune.

You can gain control of your life. You can gain clarity. You can stop feeling like you're constantly running and never getting anywhere. It starts with taming overwhelm. And to do that, you've got to start being still. So why not start now?

Project Actions

- ☑ Before turning the page to the next chapter, set a timer for 60 seconds and commit to being still.
- ☑ When the time is up, take a minute to journal on what came up for you during the stillness, what were you thinking? What were you feeling?

THE THREE STAGES OF GROWTH

What's the difference between change and growth?

Change happens whether we like it or not. Every day we're changed by what we see, hear, eat, or read. And that change can happen unintentionally, simply by existing in the world we change. It's like hair. Unless you're a member of the follically challenged crew, your hair grows. It just does, whether you want it to or not. No effort required.

Growth is different. Growth requires change, but change doesn't necessarily require growth. While passive change is often barely noticeable and requires little effort, growth requires intentional effort. And it is damn hard too! That's why even when you commit to growth, you'll give up. Because the effort can often seem too much to endure when the reward isn't certain. But if you stick with it, the person you become and the life you live on the other side of growth can be beautiful –

the discoveries you make, the things you learn, the people you meet. I want you to experience that.

So in this chapter I'm sharing with you what I call the three stages of growth. Because once you know what to expect from the growth experience, it becomes easier for you to stay the course and receive the rewards.

When clients come to work with me, when they book a strategy session, when they decide to go ahead and get started with coaching, it's because something isn't working in their life and they want to change that.

Maybe they're in a toxic job that's got them on the fast train to burnout.

Maybe they're unhappy with where they are in life, believe there has to be more, but don't know what more looks like for them.

Or maybe they're doing just fine, but they want better than fine and feel there's another level for them – there's something more that they could be doing, that they want to be doing.

We then have the call, the strategy session, where they get a taste of what coaching with me will look like, walk away with some quick wins, and then sign up to work together.

The first few sessions are a trip, especially if they've never worked with a coach before. Their mind is blown by their increased self-awareness and reframing of the age-old negative narratives they'd been telling themselves, and they feel inspired and motivated to change. They feel this way because it's all new to them. They're seeing situations differently; they're seeing themselves differently, and their idea of what's possible for them is becoming more expansive.

They're meeting with somebody (me!) for an hour every week, someone who is wholly focused on their needs, their desires, their success; no judgement, no shaming, and no agenda except to see them win, whatever winning means to them.

Now, I don't know about you, but before I started working with a coach, I'd never had that. An entire hour focused on me and what I wanted to work through. Sure, you may seek the counsel of your closest friends, but it's a different vibe. Because when you're at the point where you're questioning your life as it is and thinking of shaking things up and doing something different, you can have the most supportive friend in the world, but a friend will give you advice, and that advice is going to be tainted with their own ideas, their own vision of what they believe is possible for you, which is likely to match what they believe is possible for them and their own agenda, which is likely to be an urge to keep you comfortable and safe, not support any radical change you may wish to make.

The difference with talking through struggles and potential life changes with a coach is that there's no doubt that they're committed solely to your success and want you to realise your full potential. They get off on witnessing your breakthroughs and watching you getting after whatever it is you want.

All of that is exciting. And it makes you feel amazing. I know, I've been there myself as a client.

Sometimes all this inspired motivation and excitement occurs after the first session, sometimes after four sessions, but it's usually early in the process and that's the first stage of growth: novelty, the brain loves dopamine. And when that dopamine hits, it makes you feel so good.

Think about the last time you did something new and started to feel a shift in your clarity or ability. It was exciting, right? New, novel. And I bet it gave you that hit.

The first time you smashed a dead lift at the gym.

The first time you closed a big deal at work.

The first time you nailed a headstand in a yoga class.

The first time you crossed the finish line after a marathon.

You do it and you feel on top of the world. It feels amazing, and every fibre of your being craves more of that feeling. That's just how it is. That's biology.

But you can't sustain that high forever, and eventually you hit an iceberg, an obstacle, and lose that feel-good feeling. This dip or crash is the second stage of growth. You're riding high on dopamine, loving life, then you hit an obstacle, a challenge, something that stops you in your tracks. And suddenly, you realise that this growth and transformation quest you started out on isn't going to be plain sailing.

This is where your sympathetic nervous system kicks in because your body's like, 'Hold up! We haven't been here before. We're going to DIIIIIIEEEEEE!!!!'

And so it does what it does best to protect itself; it gets into that fight, flight, fawn, or freeze mode aka survival mode. Anxiety kicks in, and you start to freak the fuck out. You have no idea what's happening and how to deal with it because you haven't been here before.

Imagine climbing a mountain. As you get higher up the mountain, the temperature drops, the wind gets stronger and the air gets thinner. If you're not careful, if you haven't properly prepared yourself, you can suffer from altitude sickness because your body isn't used to being that high, to being in air that thin. So when the discomfort and sickness hit you, you give up. You're forced to turn around and head back down the mountain, back to where you started.

It's the same in life. The tendency is that when you hit the gnarly, uncomfortable second stage of growth, you fall back on old habits and try to do what you've always done to get you through the darkness. And when the old ways fail to work, you give up and head back down the mountain, back to your comfort zone, back to where you started, even though where you started isn't where you wanted to be, which is why you started climbing in the first place.

But like climbing a mountain, if you prepare yourself, if you take it slowly, if you allow your body time to acclimatise to this new experience, to this thinner rarefied air, your body will be like, *OK, this is new but not unexpected. We've prepared for this and that preparation means we can keep moving forward safely and sustainably.*

This is the same for you in the second stage of growth. In the first stage, you're flying high, feeling fantastic, then you hit that iceberg.

Now, what you don't want to do is fall back on old habits and go back to doing things the same way you've always done. If you haven't prepared for this eventuality, it's exactly what you'll do because it's what you know and what feels comfortable to you.

What you want to do instead, and what you're likely to do if you've been working with a coach and developed tools, habits and strategies that serve you and where you want to go, is integrate all that you learned in that high-dopamine first stage of growth and slow down. Pause, find stillness (shout out to chapter 7), then with increased clarity, restart the process, taking smaller steps as your body gets used to being in this new environment and dealing with these new challenges. Or as your body gets used to you putting yourself out there, gets used to dealing with the fear – fear of rejection, fear of embarrassment, fear of failure, fear of what other people might say.

Now don't get it twisted, just because your body becomes acclimatised to your struggles, it doesn't mean all the fear and anxiety magically disappear. But it does mean that you'll then be able to deal with it from a place of nervous system safety. Your body won't freak out to the same extent it used to because it knows that you've done something like this before, and you didn't die, so you can do it again.

So that's the second stage of growth, what I call the messy middle. It's not pretty, it's not comfortable, but if you can push through the suck, and not quit, you'll be rewarded by reaching the third stage of growth.

The third stage is a nice place to be. It's not quite your comfort zone but getting to stage three means you didn't give up during the messiness of stage two. You persevered, got through it, learned a ton about yourself and what you're capable of, and now you feel confident in your ability to meet challenges head-on and figure them out. You don't have all the answers, but you do have greater clarity about your mission or purpose, heightened self-awareness, and an increased level of self-trust.

By stage three you've experienced the dopamine fest of stage one and the messy middle of stage two, and now you've got experience. And that's a nice place to be. But you can't get complacent because once you figure out where you're heading, where this growth quest is leading you, you won't want to stop until you've got there. So there's always going to be another level you're striving for to give you what you need to keep moving forward, meaning the cycle of growth will roll around again.

See, it's not a one-and-done thing. You don't breathe a sigh of relief the first time you successfully navigate stage two. You don't spend the rest of your life chillin' in stage three, raise a trophy above your head, and cruise into the sunset.

But what does happen is each time you go through a cycle of growth, you become stronger wiser, and better equipped to anticipate and deal with life's challenges so that the next time you find yourself in the second stage of growth, you're approaching it from a place of experience. You'll see what lies ahead, and as you start to fall into that familiar pit of despair, you'll suddenly remember, *Oh, I've been here before.* Your nervous system will freak out a little, but it won't be as intense as it was last time because you'll have the tools to reset it and the confidence to know you can overcome the obstacle in front of you because you've seen something like it before.

I'll share a taste of my initial experience of the three stages of growth. When I left BigLaw, I'd only been working with a coach for a couple of months. I was at stage one, high off dopamine at all the new things I was learning about myself and the discovery of the myriad of possibilities that were available to me outside of the mental cell I'd previously felt stuck in. I'd found the keys to that mental cell of self-limitation, and I was loving the feeling of being on the outside, carving a brand-new path for myself, and the anticipation of what was yet to come.

And then as I started to figure out what I wanted to do and where I wanted to go, I realised there was a whole lot I didn't know.

I didn't know that simply training as a yoga teacher and starting an Instagram account sharing my story wasn't in itself going to help the people I wanted to help and get me to where I wanted to get to.

I didn't know sharing my story would be so hard. As I've said before, I would agonise for days or weeks over posts, worrying whether they said the right thing or hit the right tone. I worried about what people might think and say about my reinvention and candid insights. That was me entering stage two for the first time and I was stuck there for a good while. But I kept going, kept connecting to my North Star, my Why, and eventually I got through it, to stage three, which is when I was able to launch the first iteration of my podcast. In this stage I gained deeper clarity on what I wanted to say, who I wanted to say it to, and how I wanted to say it.

Then, influenced by people around me who loved what I was doing and the friends and colleagues who asked me to help, I switched gears and decided to become a coach, which began the dopamine hit of a new stage one. The cycle started again. And I've been going through these cycles periodically ever since I left BigLaw, sometimes going through all three stages in a single month!

You're probably wondering what stage I'm at now.

Well, I'd say that as I write this book, I'm firmly at stage two again. There are changes coming as I see another level of expansion and growth on the horizon for me.

There's a lot going on, decisions to be made, more layers to be shed, and I'm definitely wading through the messy middle right now. But with the work I've done, and am still doing, both alone and with the support of coaching and therapy, I'm relaxed about where I'm at because I know I've been here before and I trust I'll figure out a way through to the other side.

I know where and when to ask for support. To get the coaching, to get the therapy, to do the self-coaching and the inner work (including the practises and strategies I share in this book), to figure out what's going on and what's needed to get me to where I want to go next. And I also know that stage two is temporary. In the words of Jon Kabat-Zinn, 'You can't stop the waves, but you can learn to surf.' That's what stage two teaches you – how to surf the waves of life's ups and downs. So I'm not freaking out; I'm taking action in a way that feels aligned with the season of life and the stage of growth that I'm in right now.

I hope that this chapter has shown you that no one is immune to these three stages of growth. No one is immune to going through the yucky, horrible feelings of stage two. Growth is messy. You can take comfort in the fact that it's going to be hard, it's going to suck, but it's not going to be that way forever.

So whether you're:

- ☑ at the very beginning of your personal growth journey, thinking of making a change;
- ☑ in the dopamine fest of stage one, having opened your mental cell and become excited about the possibilities that await you;
- ☑ in stage two where you feel like nothing's working, it's all too hard, and you just want to quit and return to the life you're trying to escape from; or
- ☑ in stage three, feeling good about what you've overcome to get there and the life that lies ahead...

Wherever you are, I hope that this chapter has helped you realise that you're not alone and that everything you're experiencing right now is as it's supposed to be. Life isn't linear. And when you decide to break out of your box and start your quest back to yourself, it doesn't happen overnight. It's a never-ending process. It's a part of being alive, of thriving not just surviving. Because once you've stepped outside your mental cell, inhaled the fresh, clean air, and looked up at the sky to see there is no limit on what's possible for you, you'll never want to stop feeling that feeling. You'll never want to go back inside that cell.

So embrace every stage, feel all the feelings, and remember that whether you're currently in stage one, two or three, you're not going to be there forever.

In your workbook, journal about where you are on your growth journey. There's a prompt to guide you.

Project Actions

- ☑ Identify the stage of growth you're currently in and why.
- ☑ Think of a time you were previously at this growth stage and note down what you learned from it that can help you now.

CONNECT TO YOUR INNER CHILD
AND LET YOUR FEELINGS FLY

Have you ever been awakened by a scream?

A scream so loud and forceful that you believed the screamer must be in intense pain, maybe even dying?

If not, be grateful.

If you have, you must, like me, be a parent.

My six-year-old awoke one morning and emitted such a scream. He wasn't in pain, though, at least not physical pain. So what was the reason for this rude awakening?

He woke up to find my wife had already got out of bed to get ready for work, and he was pissed!

Now as you can probably imagine, it's annoying as hell being woken up by a blood-curdling cry, and my instinct was to tell him to stop being ridiculous. But I knew from experience that until his mum got back into bed so he could get up with her, he would make his displeasure known and continue screaming.

Amidst all the fuss, I resigned myself to the fact that I was never getting back to sleep and took my eight-year-old downstairs for breakfast. I got him the bowl of granola he politely requested, then prepared and gulped down my vitamin shake while my much-needed coffee brewed in my Bialetti stovetop coffee maker. All was well. And in that moment, I mentally declared the eight-year-old my favourite child.

Then he asked for toast.

There's a quote I read on a poster once that said 'Life's too short to drink bad wine and bad coffee.' I'd add to the list, life's too short to eat bad bread. Once you've tasted a freshly baked, additive-free loaf of sourdough from your local bakery, you can't go back. So maybe what happened next is my fault for refusing to eat bad bread and getting myself into a position where my kids will only eat the same fresh sourdough that bread dreams are made of. When I was a kid, I ate what was put in front of me, typically a standard supermarket loaf, additives and all. It was the 1980s, we didn't have much money, there was no local bakery at the end of the street and I knew no different.

But my Singapore-born bougie offspring have specific bread requirements and won't settle for anything less than, as they call it, *crunchy toast*. And they chomp through it at such a rate that I'm now on first name terms with the people in the bakery and have my very own loyalty card.

Anyway, I thought I was prepared for the toast request. But when I went to get the bread from the bread bin on the kitchen counter, the loaf was almost done! Still, there was just enough bread for the little prince to have two slices, or so I thought as I slid them in the toaster.

Boy, was I wrong!

The toast popped up; I spread on the requested vegan butter and Marmite and presented the plate to his royal highness.

Then all hell broke loss!

You would have thought I'd taken the contents of the rubbish bin and served it to him by how he reacted. Screaming and jumping up and down like a overexcited kangaroo.

What was my crime?

One slice of toast was smaller than the other.

FFS!

By that point, I'd had it with my darling children. I took my coffee (can you believe all of this occurred before any caffeine had touched my lips and hit my blood stream?!) to the living room, shut the door, and employed the meditation and stillness techniques mentioned in this book to prevent the rage bubbling inside me from spilling over.

Good f***in' morning.

I was mad with both kids then and told them, in no uncertain terms, how ridiculous and unacceptable their behaviour was. But once they were safely deposited at school, I returned home to my zen den and reflected on the morning's shenanigans. And in my reflection, I saw that in their own way, they were doing exactly what I invite my clients to do.

No, not throw tantrums because you didn't wake up next to the person you wanted to, or your toast was the wrong size. That's annoying in a child but downright weird in an adult. What I invite and encourage them to do is express their feelings fully and have the courage to advocate for what they want.

In the calm after the storm, I could see things differently.

My six-year-old was annoyed and probably anxious that his mother wasn't next to him when he woke up. That's what he expected and wanted. When he didn't get what he wanted, instead of doing what we're conditioned to do – suppress our feelings and pretend everything's fine – he made his feelings known, clearly and forcefully stating what he wanted and expected.

My eight-year-old expected toast of equal size. That's what he wanted. When he didn't get that, he let it be known he wasn't happy and argued his case. He didn't simply settle; he didn't say, 'OK, it's not what I want, but I'll just eat it anyway' to be polite (although that would have been nice). He raised hell! Both kids let their feelings fly.

Now, don't get me wrong. The behaviour exhibited by both kids was awful. There are valid reasons that explain it to some degree, reasons that I won't go into here, but don't believe for a second that I'm in any way condoning it.

I'm sharing this story because I want you to momentarily put yourself in a child's shoes and think back to a recent situation where you did something you didn't want to do because you felt you should or you had to.

Maybe it was taking on a task at work that was dumped on you because nobody else volunteered, doing a favour for a family member who never does anything for you, or going to an event with a friend when you'd have much rather stayed home.

Why did you do it?

Were you trying to be polite?

Maybe you were trying to enhance your career prospects.

Maybe you were trying to keep the peace.

Maybe you didn't want to upset your friend.

How did it make you feel? Unhappy? Resentful? Angry? And did you express those feelings? Or did you suppress them because that's what you're supposed to do, and you were scared of what people might say?

OK, replay that scenario again but through the lens of a child. And if, like me, you were a good child who never did anything wrong,[24] use my kids as your model. How would you have dealt with that situation differently?

Would you have done the thing you didn't want to do? Or would you have stood strong and boldly said, 'No! I don't want to.'

How does it make you feel when you visualise yourself saying no? Advocating for yourself and making it clear what you want.

It probably feels scary.

But does it also feel a little empowering? I bet it does.

And this is what happens when you find yourself. You get to know yourself on a deeper level. Your wants, needs, and desires. You get to know what it feels like to live life Lit! You get super attuned to the things that dampen that spark within you.

---

[24] OK, this may be the second lie in this book.

And with that knowledge of self comes strength and courage, allowing you to push past the fear of disappointing people, ditch the persona of people-pleaser, and be intentional about what you say *yes* to and what you say *no* to.

So the next time you're asked to do something that makes your heart drop or accept something you know you don't want, ask yourself, what would my inner child do?

Then do that.

But maybe leave out the screaming and bouncing part!

Complete the inner child exercise in your workbook.

Project Actions

- ☑ Think of a situation where you did something you didn't want to do and resented doing it or ended up embroiled in a situation that didn't serve you.
- ☑ Replay the situation from the standpoint of your inner child. How could you have handled the situation differently?

10
FIND THE KEYS AND SET YOURSELF FREE

The black SUV pulled out of Bali airport and hit the traffic-clogged highway. It was late December and we were heading to a pimped-out villa in Canggu for a well-deserved Christmas holiday with friends. From the online photos the villa looked out of this world! Pool, multiple bathrooms, gym, full-time staff including a chef! This holiday was going to rock!

But as a BigLaw lawyer, your life is never fully your own, on holiday, or even at Christmas. I'd been reprimanded once for having my phone off when I was away on leave at a family wedding, so even though it was Christmas and even though I'd wrapped up any loose ends before leaving the office back in Singapore, I knew I had to do the obligatory post-flight phone check.

As we sat in gridlocked traffic, the cool air of the SUV's aircon protecting us from the Balinese heat, I pressed the button on my work iPhone and felt that familiar feeling of anxiety and dread as I waited for it to boot up and connect to the network.

I stared at the screen as it changed from black to showing the white Apple logo, then to the lock screen, the suspense of what awaited me once this unwanted gift was unwrapped hanging heavily in the air. And as my device connected to the local network and emails began to flood my inbox, I noticed it, the all too familiar subject line. It was the name of a deal that had taken a lot of my time that year but had gone unexpectedly quiet a couple of months prior.

Yet, with spectacularly inconvenient timing, I was now reading an email from my client informing me that the deal had returned from the dead ... with an accelerated timeline.

Target closing date ... 31 December. Less than two weeks away.

Despite the coolness of the SUV's aircon, I was now sweating profusely as a cocktail of emotions that included anger and frustration flooded my body. In an instant the joy and excitement of a Christmas holiday in one of my favourite places was replaced with the all too familiar realisation that this holiday would now be a working one.

And so it was.

Moments of fun with family and friends were interspersed with frequent moments locked in the spare room of the villa, which became my makeshift office. I took calls, responded to emails, and reviewed and drafted documents to the soundtrack of the fun and games happening in and around the villa. You haven't lived until you've led an all-party call and negotiated documents on Christmas Eve!

And even in the moments outside of that spare room, the deal took up valuable real estate in my brain making it difficult to switch off, be present and fully enjoy the holiday.

Predictably, 31 December came and went without the deal closing.

And it was on the flight back to Singapore that I admitted I'd reached my enough point. The point at which I knew I didn't want this life. The point at which I knew I had to leave BigLaw.

Yes, the BigLaw life had afforded me this amazing trip to Bali. But it had robbed me of so much more.

My time.

My well-being.

My sense of purpose.

On the flight home I vowed my life had to change. I'd said similar things before, but the weight of my limiting beliefs and fear had always held me back, keeping me in my mental cell. But as I gazed out of the airplane window, I knew this time was different. I envisioned my life five years from that point and I knew I didn't want what I saw. Something had to change. And change would only happen if I made it happen.

That's when my plan to escape my box began.

Well, I say plan, but really there was no plan. Only a desire and a deep-rooted need to shake my life up, to get out of the funk I'd been in, to stop being confined to a box I believed I couldn't break out of and challenge my idea of what could be possible for me.

That desire has fuelled me ever since and led to my life changing in ways I couldn't have imagined. And with each change, each win, each milestone, my belief in what's possible changes.

I no longer feel confined to a box, accepting that where or what I am is where or what I'll always have to be.

I no longer feel I've absentmindedly got on a train that's heading to someplace I don't want to go to.

I know my place, I know my purpose, and I have my peace.

And that's what I want for you.

To be so clear about who you are, what you want, and why you want it.

To be so confident in your ability to figure things out that you trust and believe you can get what you want.

To be so damn courageous that each and every day you take action to get after what you want.

I want your life to not just be something you survive as you tick off the evergrowing list of 'shoulds', but a wild, enjoyable, thrilling ride where you thrive.

That's why I do the work I do and it's why I wrote this book.

To get you rethinking how you approach and live your life.

Why you believe the things that you believe.

Why you do things the way you do them.

Are you living the way you imagined you'd live, the way you want to live, and if not, why? What needs to change and how will you change it so that can happen?

One of the most common phrases I hear from clients is, 'I've never thought it about that way before.' And I love it!

I love it because that's the catalyst for change. When you begin to question a common thought, perceived reality, or way of seeing the world, it starts a process that cannot help but change you.

So as you come to the end of this book, I encourage you to take a few moments to think about what's shifted for you.

What chapter left you thinking, *I've never thought about it that way before*?

What story made you stop and think differently about what's possible for you?

What question unlocked an idea that has you excited about a new direction or has made you realise you've reached your enough point?

Your answers to these questions are the keys to your mental cell of self-limitation. So go ahead, work through the workbook and reread this book as often as you need so you can find those keys, unlock the door, and escape your box so you can find your place, purpose, and peace in the world.

ACKNOWLEDGEMENTS

I recorded the first draft of the introduction to this book as a voice note on my iPhone as I stood on a beach in Whitby, a town in the north of England. So, it's fitting that I close this book by writing these acknowledgments while sat on the beach at Bigbury-on-Sea on the South West coast of the England.

At the time of writing, I've just read through the thoughtful, insightful and valuable feedback on the near final draft of this book from my beta readers so thanking these awesome humans seems a good place to start.

Thank you for your kind, supportive and honest feedback and for giving up your time to read my words and help make this book better. It was especially heartwarming to know that certain aspects of the book helped each of you in addressing situations happening in your own lives at the time of reading. Thank you for sharing.

Thank you to to my book coach and developmental editor, Pia Edberg, copy editor, Catherine Turner and book designer, Ines Monnet, for making this book look and read as good as the first one. It was great to work with each of you again, see you for book 3?

Thanks to Karolina Wudniak for nailing the brief and designing a cover that pops!

Thanks to each and every one of my coaching clients for placing your trust in me as your coach and affording me the privilege of supporting you on your quest to find your place, purpose and peace in the world.

To my boys, Luca & Rafa, thanks for being constant reminders to me to connect with my inner child. And to my wife, Hazel thank you for being you.

Finally, thank you to you, the reader. I'm a firm believer that people don't find books, books find people, so I know this book found you for a reason. I'm thankful it did and I truly hope you are too. Boxes are for products not people so my wish is that you escape your box and go find the things you're meant to do and live the life you're meant to live. I'll be here cheering you on.

THREE REQUESTS

Thank you for reading this book. Before you go and get to work on the workbook, I have the following three requests:

- ☑ Don't put this book back on the shelf and forget about it. Implement what you've learned and do something differently today. Make a different decision, decide to think a different thought, take a different action that supports the path you're carving for yourself and the person you're becoming (or want to become).

- ☑ Share this book with a friend, colleague or family member who's feeling stuck right now so they can unlock their mental cell of self-limitation and find their place, purpose and peace.

- ☑ Leave a review where you bought this book. Your words matter, to me, but more importantly to the people like you that are looking for a book like this. Your review could be the difference between someone picking up this book and escaping a soul sucking existence or staying stuck in the status quo and never realising and creating the life they want to live. So please, don't underestimate the power of your review, however long or short it maybe.

ABOUT THE AUTHOR

Ryan Spence is a life coach, yoga teacher, author of the corporate coaching guide, The Triple C Method® and a former BigLaw lawyer.

A first-class law graduate of the University of London, Ryan's prestigious eleven-year career in BigLaw involved him in deals that won the Finance Deal of the Year at the 2018 Asia Legal Awards and the 2019 UN Global Impact Award.

When Ryan realised that each rung of the corporate ladder he reached was taking him further from where he wanted to be, he took a leap of faith and set off on a quest to find himself. Driven by his own experience of corporate life, Ryan has become a passionate leader in the corporate wellbeing and mindset sphere, coaching professionals to find their version of fulfilment, meaning and joy so they can move from survival mode to thrival mode and live life Lit!

Having previously lived in London and Singapore, Ryan currently resides in Sheffield in the UK.

To book Ryan for speaking engagements, interviews or yoga events, email: hey@iamryanspence.com

WWW.IAMRYANSPENCE.COM

@IAM_RYANSPENCE

ASK ME ANYTHING

www.ingramcontent.com/pod-product-compliance
Lightning Source LLC
Chambersburg PA
CBHW030554080526
44585CB00012B/374